Bible Stories

(Originally Titled THE YOUNG PEOPLE'S BOOK OF BIBLE STORIES)

Publishers · GROSSET & DUNLAP · New York
A FILMWAYS COMPANY

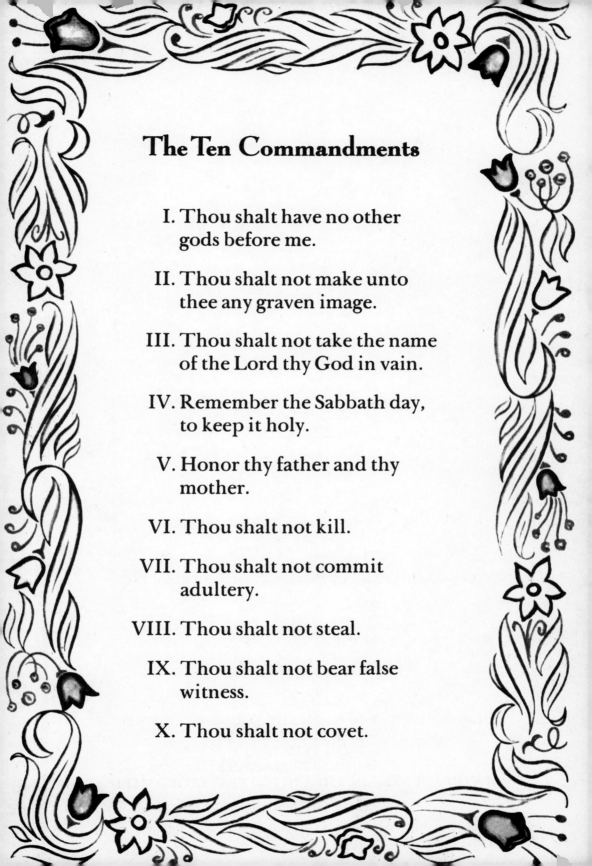

The Ten Commandments

I. Thou shalt have no other gods before me.

II. Thou shalt not make unto thee any graven image.

III. Thou shalt not take the name of the Lord thy God in vain.

IV. Remember the Sabbath day, to keep it holy.

V. Honor thy father and thy mother.

VI. Thou shalt not kill.

VII. Thou shalt not commit adultery.

VIII. Thou shalt not steal.

IX. Thou shalt not bear false witness.

X. Thou shalt not covet.

God's Fingerprints

by CHARLES M. SHELDON

Author of *In His Steps*

AVE you ever sat in a car near the curb in a big city and watched the people as they passed? If you have done this, you have noticed that no two persons are alike. Each person has a different face; no two have exactly the same kind of nose or forehead or chin. All are different.

If you could take the fingerprints of all these strangers you would find, too, that each of them has fingerprints of his own—fingerprints like those of no one else in the world. And then you would realize more than ever how different are all the people who are alive today.

But think of all the fingerprints that God has made since the day of the Creation! And think how each of them has represented a single person—a king, a slave, a mother, a thief, a child, an old man, a shepherd boy, an explorer, a scientist, a business man!

You have heard that the Bible is the most wonderful book in the world. It tells the stories of many, many "fingerprints"—not imaginary people, not strange or dull ones, but people who had hopes and fears, joys and griefs, just like ours. The more we read about them the more we understand that, although they are all interesting and different, they are all human like us. Woodrow Wilson was right when he called the Bible the "word of life," a book peopled by thousands of real men and women and children.

The people of the Bible lived long ago. Jesus himself never saw a church, a public school, an airplane, a subway, a telephone, a printing press, or many other things that we all are familiar with today. Few if any of the Bible's people could have imagined such things as the motion picture or radio or electric light. Yet when we read about them we feel close to them; it does not seem to matter that they lived thousands of years ago. Like us, they know what it is to be alive.

And that is why Bible stories such as the ones to be found in this book will never grow old. They are the stories of people who were God's children as we are, who chose between right and wrong day by day, who had in their hearts the thoughts and feelings that make life happy or unhappy, worthwhile or useless. These people are all different, but they are all God's fingerprints.

Many people of the Bible were heroes and heroines, and the stories of their lives should inspire us today. As you read these stories you will see how men and women and children of long ago struggled for what they believed was good, and were rewarded. This is possible for us today as it was for them. For we, too, are fingerprints of God.

Contents

THE OLD TESTAMENT

THE NEW TESTAMENT

Adam and Eve in Paradise

OD is a Being powerful, wise, and good above every other. He made the heavens, and the earth, and all things that are in them.

There were no people upon this earth at first; neither did any thing grow upon it. It was not even shaped into its present form; and darkness was all around it. But God created the light, and the blue sky overhead. He made the seas and the dry land, the sun, the moon, and the stars. And in the seas He made great whales, and every kind of fish that swims in the waters. And He commanded the earth to bring forth grass, and trees bearing fruit, and plants yielding all manner of seed; and it did so. Then He created the birds and the beasts, and every thing that He had made was very good. Last of all, He made man in His own image, and blessed him, and gave to him all the whole earth, with its fruits and living creatures for him to use and enjoy.

All these things God did in six days; and on the seventh day He rested from His work. So He blessed the seventh day, and called it a holy day.

The first man and woman whom God created were

called Adam and Eve. The name signifies "earth," for he was formed out of the dust of the ground. Eve means "life," and she was so called because she was the "mother of all living." And God placed the man and the woman in a beautiful garden which He had made for them in Eden, bidding them cultivate it, and keep it in good order. In this garden were all kinds of trees; not only those that were lovely to look at, but others bearing fruit for them to eat. But there was one tree in the midst of the garden, called the Tree of Knowledge of Good and Evil, of whose fruit God commanded them not to eat, because if they did so they should die. Of every other fruit He gave them leave to eat freely.

Then God brought together all the birds and beasts that He had created, that Adam might gives names to them. And whatever Adam called each one, that was its name.

So these two, Adam and Eve, lived happily in this garden of Eden, or Paradise, as it is also called; for they did what God commanded them, and He loved them.

Eve and the serpent.

Adam and Eve Driven Out of Paradise

BUT Adam and Eve did not remain long in the garden of Eden. They sinned against the good God, who had given them not only it, but so many other beautiful things. And then, as God had said, death came upon them, and their children after them. They were also punished by being put out of the garden. The manner of it was this:

The Serpent one day spoke to Eve, asking her whether God had indeed forbidden them to eat the fruit of some of the trees in the garden. She answered him that they might eat of every one, save that of the Tree of Knowledge of Good and Evil, which grew in the midst of the garden. Of that God had said they must not eat, for if they did they should die. But the Serpent told her that was not true; they would not die if they ate of it, for God had forbidden it only because He knew that if they did eat of it they should become equal to Himself, knowing good and evil.

Eve listened to the Serpent while he told her this lie, for such it was. She saw how beautiful the fruit was, and she wanted to become wise, as the Serpent had told her she should; so at length, heedless of God's having forbidden it, she picked and ate it; and Adam, who was with her, did the same.

But no sooner had they eaten it than they knew they had done wrong; and in the cool of the day, when they heard the voice of the Lord God in the garden, they hid themselves among the trees that He might not see them. But God called them, and, afraid though they were, they were obliged to come before Him. And when He asked them why they were afraid, and had hidden themselves, they had to confess what they had done: that they had allowed the Serpent to persuade them to eat of the fruit which God had forbidden.

God was greatly displeased with them for their disobedience. And after telling them what sad things should happen to them through it, He drove them out of the garden into the rough, rugged world, where thorns and thistles were to grow because of their sin; and where with toil and difficulty they should procure their own sustenance, in place of eating the fruit which He had given them in Eden. Then he clothed them with the skins of beasts; for, though angry with them, He had pity on their forlorn condition; and, putting them out of the garden, a wonderful guard of angels was placed there, that none should approach the Tree of Life.

Cain and Abel

AFTER they left the garden of Eden Adam and Eve had two sons called Cain and Abel. Cain, the elder, was a husbandman, that is, one who cultivates the ground; Abel, the younger, was a shepherd.

In those days it was the will of God that men should offer sacrifices to Him; and these two brought each his offering: Cain brought of the fruits of the earth, while Abel offered the best of his flocks. With Abel's offering God was pleased, because it was one which He Himself had commanded. But He was not pleased with the offering that Cain brought, because it was one which He had not commanded, and because Cain had brought it in place of that which he knew was required of him. In this he was disobedient to God, as his parents had been in the garden; and he was angry when he saw that his offering was not accepted. God, however, was patient with him and told him that if he brought that which was commanded, his offering should even then be accepted, and He would be pleased with him, as He had been with Abel.

But, instead of giving heed to what God said to him, Cain

went away and quarreled with his brother; and his anger against him rose to such a height, that presently, when they were in the field together, he fell upon him and killed him!

Then God himself called unto Cain, "Where is Abel, thy brother?" and Cain answered, "I know not; am I my brother's keeper?" But his lying could not conceal his wicked deed from God. He had seen all that passed in the field when Cain had killed his brother; and now He told him that he was accursed for this cruel murder; that from that time his labor in cultivating the ground should be in vain, for it should yield nothing to him; that he should be driven out from his family and his country; and that for the rest of his life he should be a wanderer on the face of the earth. Cain did not express any sorrow for what he had done when God pronounced this curse upon him. He only cried out that his punishment was greater than he could bear; and he feared lest any one who knew why he was condemned to wander about in that wretched manner should kill him for having killed his brother.

But God told him that his life should be spared. And He set a certain mark upon Cain, that all who saw it should know that God had appointed him, not to be killed, but to live—a miserable murderer!

Noah Builds the Ark

ADAM and Eve had other sons besides Cain and Abel. They had daughters also; and, as time passed on, many hundreds of years, their descendants peopled the earth. But men then became exceedingly wicked; so much so, that God was sorry that He had ever made them. And at length, seeing they would not amend their ill-doings, though He gave them opportunity for amendment, He determined to destroy them, together with all the living creatures that were upon the earth.

There was, however, one good man, named Noah, among these wicked people; and it was God's will to save him from the flood of waters with which he was about to drown the whole world, with its inhabitants. So He told Noah to prepare an Ark, that is, a kind of boat, large enough to contain himself and his family, together with two of every kind of living creatures, birds, beasts, and even creeping things; besides food for them to eat till the waters should have passed away from off the earth. God told him precisely how he was to build the Ark, what size it was to be, how it was to be shaped, how many stories there were to be in it, where the door was to be placed; and that he must cover it with pitch, inside and out, to keep out the water. And Noah did all as God commanded him.

So great a vessel was long in building; and day after day, as Noah and his sons worked at it, their neighbors saw what they were doing, and Noah warned them of their danger. But they heeded him not. So at length, when the time came beyond which God would not wait for their repentance the Ark was finished. Noah and his family and all the creatures that were to be kept alive with him, went into it, and God shut them in.

Then, for forty days and forty nights, God poured out rain from heaven, the waves of the great deep were dashed violently upon the dry land, and the waters rose till it was all one vast sea. Still they kept rising, higher and higher, so that at last even the tops of the loftiest mountains were covered; and every living creature that was left upon the earth perished in that dreadful flood.

But Noah, and all that were shut up with him, escaped, as God had appointed; for the Ark sailed safely along upon the waters.

Noah Gives Thanks to God

FOR a hundred and fifty days the waters of the deluge covered the earth. Then God caused them to abate; for He stopped the rain, and quieted the great waves of the sea, and sent a strong wind upon the earth, and at length the Ark rested upon the mountains of Ararat in Armenia.

But, though the tops of the high mountains appeared above the waters, the land around was still like a sea, so that Noah could not yet leave the Ark. Then, after waiting forty days, seeing the flood continue to abate, he opened the window of the Ark, and sent out a raven and a dove, that he might know whether the waters had dried up or not. The poor dove flew hither and thither; but, finding no resting-place, for the waters were still all abroad, returned to Noah, who put out his hand and drew her in to him. Seven days after he sent her forth again, and in the evening she flew back, having in her mouth an olive-leaf newly plucked off; by which Noah knew that the dry land had at last appeared. Again he waited seven days, and then again sent out the dove. But this time she did not come back; and Noah removed the covering of the Ark, and saw that the ground was quite dry.

Then, after they had been shut up in it a whole year, God commanded him and his family, and all the living creatures that were with him, to come out of the Ark; and when they did so, Noah built an altar, and offered upon it such a sacrifice as God had appointed. And God was pleased with it, and blessed Noah, and all human beings that should come after him; saying that He would not again curse the ground, as He had done before, for Adam's sin in Eden, neither would He any more destroy the world by a flood. And again He gave the earth, and all that it contains, to man, as He had in the beginning given it to Adam in Paradise.

The rainbow which is seen in the clouds after rain was appointed by God Himself as a token or sign of His promise that He would never again destroy the world by a flood; for He told Noah that, whenever it should appear in the cloud, He would look upon it, and remember that He had made this promise to His creatures.

Noah was six hundred years old when the deluge came upon the earth, and he lived three hundred and fifty years after it; so he was nine hundred and fifty years old when he died.

The Tower of Babel

OW the three sons of Noah,—Shem, Ham, and Japheth, had many children, and all these had children too, for God had commanded them to multiply and people the earth. So, as time went on, there were multitudes of people all descended from Noah, and they all dwelt together, and the whole earth spoke the same language and had the same way of life.

After a time they travelled from the east, all this great body of people together, and they found a plain in the land of Shinar. It pleased them very much, and they stopped their wanderings and settled down there.

But God had not intended them to settle down all in the same place. He wanted them to spread and people the whole earth.

They said to one another, "Go to, let us make brick and burn them thoroughly."

Then they used the brick for stone and slime or wet mud for mortar, and they began to build.

They said, "Let us build a city and a tower, whose top

ST. JOHN THE BAPTIST'S TOMB
IN SEBASTIA.

THE STORY OF THE PICTURE
(on inside pages)

THE CHILDREN OF ISRAEL ENTER THE PROMISED LAND
(Deut. 34: 1-4, 7-8)

Forty years of struggle against bondage enabled the children of Israel to overcome hardships of the wilderness and the hostility of their enemies. They are about to attain the desired goal for which they have been striving through weary years of sorrow and suffering. Moses stands upon a rocky elevation from which he can see the Promised Land in the distance and, although he will never enter this land, he has faithfully brought his people to its gates. Joshua will soon take command. He stands with his hand placed affectionately on the shoulder of the aged Moses, and looks upon him with respect and admiration.

The children of Israel press forward eagerly. Many of them, however, are sorrowful about leaving their beloved leader and they pause briefly to cast a farewell glance; but all of them are imbued with gratitude, hope, and expectancy.

VALLEY OF TEARS BETWEEN NAZARETH AND JERUSALEM.

may reach unto heaven; and let us make us a name, lest we be scattered abroad upon the face of the whole earth."

The Lord came down to see the city and the tower, which had been built by the children of men.

And the Lord said, "Behold, the people is one, and they all have one language. This they begin to do, and now nothing will be restrained from them, which they have imagined to do."

"Go to, let us go down, and there confuse their language, so that they may not understand one another's speech."

So the Lord went down and scattered the people upon the face of all the earth. And He confused their language so that they could not understand one another. The tower and the city were unfinished, and the name of it was called Babel.

Abram, Son of God

IN Ur of the Chaldees, lived one of the descendants of Shem, Noah's oldest son. His name was Terah, and he had three sons—Abram, Nahor, and Haran.

Terah moved with his sons and his family from Ur of the Chaldees to Haran, and they lived there together until Terah died.

Then the Lord spoke to Abram, and He said, "Go out of this country, and away from your people and your father's house, to a land which I will show you.

"And I will make you the founder of a great nation, I will bless you, and make your name great. I will bless them that bless you, and I will curse them that curse you, and in you shall all families of the earth be blessed."

Abraham was seventy-five years old when God spoke to him. He took Sarai his wife, and Lot, who was his nephew, with him, and they went forth into the land of Canaan. When they reached Sichem, the Lord again appeared to Abram and said to him:

"Unto thy seed will I give this land."

Abram travelled southward, past Bethel, and he built

there an altar to the Lord. A famine came upon the land, and Abram had to go still farther southward, to Egypt, to escape it; and he lived in Egypt for some time. But at length he came back to Bethel, to the very place where he had built his first altar. Lot was with him, but they did not stay together very long.

Lot's Wife

IN the land of Canaan, which is in the eastern part of the world, where God first placed human beings, lived a man whose name was Lot. He was the nephew of Abram, whom God Himself had bidden to go and live there; telling him that he should become the founder of a great nation, and that, through him, blessing should come upon the whole race of man.

Abram and Lot were both so very rich, not only in gold and silver, but in flocks of sheep and herds of cattle, that the country where they dwelt was not large enough for them to live in comfortably; and owing to this, their servants, who tended the cattle, quarreled. Abram was very wishful that there should be peace between himself and his nephew; so he proposed that they should separate, one going in this direction, and the other in that; offering to Lot the first choice of land, while he himself would take what was left. Accordingly, Lot chose the plain of the River Jordan, a rich, well-watered country, and went away to it, pitching his tent near the city of Sodom.

But the people who lived in that city were wicked beyond

expression; and when God could no longer endure their wickedness, He determined to destroy both them and their city by fire from heaven. Lot, however, was a good man, and, that he might not perish among the wicked people of Sodom, two angels were sent to bid him and all his household leave that place. Lot did not know that they were angels: he thought they were two travelers on their way; so when he saw them, as he sat, in the evening, at the gate of Sodom, he rose to meet them, and begged them to come into his house for food and rest that night, and the next day they should continue their journey. The angels came in, and after they had eaten they told him that he must immediately get out of the city, for God was about to destroy it for its wickedness. And as Lot lingered, unwilling to leave his home, they laid hold of him, with his wife and daughters, and compelled them to flee for their lives; bidding them neither look behind them nor loiter upon the plain, but escape at once to the mountain. Then God rained down fire and brimstone upon Sodom and Gomorrah, and utterly destroyed them, with all their inhabitants.

But as they were fleeing, Lot's wife disregarded the command of the angels; and looking behind her, as if to return to the city she had left, she was, for her disobedience, turned into a pillar of salt.

Hagar and Ishmael

WHEN Abram, the uncle of Lot, was ninety-nine years old (for men lived much longer then than they do now), God appeared to him, and told him, as He had done before, that great multitudes of people should descend from him, and that He would give to him, and his children after him, the whole land of Canaan, in which he was then living. And He changed his name to Abraham, which means the "Father of many nations."

Abraham had at this time one son, named Ishmael, and he thought that he should inherit the things that God had promised. But God revealed to him that his son Isaac, who was not then born, should be his heir. Ishmael, however, was to become a great prince, and God pronounced a blessing upon him.

Isaac was born about a year afterward. When he was weaned, Abraham made a great entertainment for his friends; and on this occasion, Ishmael, who was about fourteen years old, behaved in a very improper and disrespectful manner. Very likely, as the elder, he thought rather too much was made of the little child, on whose account the entertainment was given. Sarah, Isaac's mother, saw his ill conduct, and was so angry that she desired Abraham to send both Ishmael and his mother Hagar from home. Abraham was unwilling to do so, for he loved Ishmael; but God told him to send them away, as Sarah had said, for He would take care of Isaac. So, early in the morning, he gave Hagar some food and water, and sent her and the boy away.

Poor Hagar wandered about in the wilderness of Beer-sheba. Very soon the water was all done, and, thinking her son must die with thirst, she laid him down in the shade of some bushes, going herself a little distance off, that she might not see him die. There she sat weeping. But an angel called to her out of heaven, asking her why she wept; and, bidding her not fear, told her that God had heard the voice of the forsaken Ishmael, and would save him.

Then Hagar, looking up, saw she was near a well of water; so she filled her empty bottle, and took drink to the lad, whose life was thus saved.

Ishmael grew up stout and strong, and became a great archer, living in the wilderness of Arabia, where his descendants were afterward a numerous people.

Abraham and Isaac

ABRAHAM loved his son Isaac very much: now that Ishmael was gone, he was his only child. And then he loved Isaac the more, because he looked forward to the time when the covenant (that is, a solemn promise) that God had made with him of greatness to his descendants, and good to all mankind, should be fulfilled in Isaac.

When Isaac was grown up to be a young man, the love and obedience which Abraham professed to God were put to a strange and terrible proof. God himself commanded him to take this only son, whom he loved, to a distant country, and there offer him up as a burnt-offering! It was indeed a strange and terrible command. But Abraham knew that God must be obeyed, and he did not for a moment delay doing as he was told, bitter though it was to him. So he rose early the next morning, prepared the wood for the burnt-offering, and, taking two of his servants with him, set out with Isaac on his journey to the land of Moriah, the place to which God had directed him.

For three days they traveled onward, and at last the mountain on which the sacrifice was to be offered was seen in the distance. Abraham then bade his servants stay behind, while he and Isaac went to the mountain to worship God; and, giving Isaac the wood to carry, he himself taking fire and a knife, they went on together.

As they went, Isaac, who did not know the command which his father had received, asked Abraham what all these preparations meant. "Father," he said, "here is fire and the wood, but where is the lamb for a burnt-offering?" Abraham could not tell him that "he" was to be the sacrifice. So he answered, "My son, God will provide himself a lamb for a burnt-offering."

When they reached the place to which God had sent them, Abraham built an altar, and laid Isaac his son bound upon it. But just when he was about to kill him, an angel called to Abraham out of heaven, bidding him not to slay his son, for God had given him the command only to see whether he would obey Him, when obedience was a hard and painful thing to him. And, in reward for his willingness to obey, God again blessed him, as He had done before.

Then, looking up, Abraham saw a ram caught by its horns in a thicket. And he took that, and offered it for a sacrifice instead of his son.

Rebekah at the Well

WHEN Isaac was about forty years of age, Abraham, who was then a very old man, wished that his son, who was to inherit all his possessions, should be married. But, as he was unwilling that Isaac should marry any one of the families of Canaan, where he lived, he bade his chief servant, or steward, go into Mesopotamia, the country whence Abraham had come into Canaan, and there, according to the custom of those times, choose a wife for Isaac from among his own relations, and bring her back with him.

The servant was afraid that she whom he chose might not be willing to return with him to a strange country; and he asked Abraham whether, in that case, he must take Isaac to her. Abraham replied to him that he believed God would give him success in his errand; but, even if it were not so, Isaac must on no account go thither himself. So the servant took ten camels, which were the usual beasts of burden in that country, and at once set out on his journey, carrying with him presents—ornaments of gold, and other precious things, for her whom he should choose for Isaac's wife.

When he came into Mesopotamia, to the city where Nahor, Abraham's brother, lived, he stopped to water his camels at a well outside the city. Now in those days it was the custom even for women of rank to go to the wells to draw water; and on that evening, just as the camels had kneeled down to drink, Rebekah, Nahor's granddaughter, came to the well with her pitcher on her shoulder. The servant went to meet her, and asked her to let him drink from the pitcher. She answered him courteously, and, letting down the pitcher from her shoulder, bade him drink, saying she would also draw water for the camels. Then, emptying the pitcher into the trough, she ran again to the well, and drew till the camels had all had enough. The man stood wondering at this, for, before she came up, he had prayed to God that the woman whom he ought to choose for Isaac's wife might do as Rebekah had done. Then he put upon her some of the jewels he had brought with him, asking her whose daughter she was, and whether there was room in her father's house for him to lodge. And when he heard that she was the daughter of Bethuel, Abraham's nephew, he gave thanks to God for having brought him to his master's family, and for the kindness with which he had been treated.

Isaac and Rebekah

REBEKAH bade the servant welcome to her father's house, and then she hastened home and told all that had befallen her at the well. Her brother Laban, seeing the jewels which the man had given to her, immediately went out and brought him and the men that were with him into the house. Then, when the camels had been ungirthed and fed, and water had been brought to wash the feet of the travelers, as is the custom in the East, food was set before them.

But the servant would not eat till he had told who he was and on what business he came. He said that he was servant to Abraham, whom God had greatly blessed, giving him many flocks, and herds, and servants, with much gold and silver; and that he had been sent to that country to choose a wife for his master's son, Isaac, who was to inherit all his father's riches. He told also how he had prayed to God at the well that He would point out to him whom he should choose for Isaac's wife; and that Rebekah had done all that he had asked in his prayer. And then he bade them say at once whether they would let Rebekah go to be Isaac's wife; for, if not, he must seek one for him elsewhere.

They answered him that they would willingly consent to let her go; so in the morning, when he and his cattle were rested and refreshed, the servant was anxious to set out immediately. Her mother and her brother, however, objected to this; they did not like to part with her so soon. But the man was in haste to return to his master; so Rebekah was sent for, and, as she was willing, they at once began their journey; she, and her nurse, and women-servants, riding upon the camels that Abraham's servant had brought with him.

One evening, as they traveled on, Rebekah, raising her eyes, saw a man coming to meet them. She asked who it was; and, when Abraham's servant told her it was his master's son, Isaac, she alighted from her camel to receive him, wrapped closely in her veil, or mantle, according to the custom of Eastern women. When they met, the servant told Isaac all that had happened to him on his journey. And then Isaac took Rebekah home to his mother's tent, and married her; and the love that he had for her comforted him for his mother's death.

Abraham lived till nearly forty years after this; and when he died, his sons, Isaac and Ishmael, buried him in the cave of Machpelah with Sarah his wife.

Isaac Blessing Jacob

ISAAC had two sons, twin brothers, called Esau and and Jacob. Esau, the elder, passed his life in the wild, open country, hunting. He was his father's favorite. Jacob lived quietly in tents, tending his flocks and herds; and his mother loved him best.

As they grew up, the brothers did not agree very well. On two occasions Jacob treated Esau with great injustice, and even cruelty. One day Esau came in from hunting, faint with hunger, and, seeing Jacob with food before him, begged him to give him some. This Jacob refused to do, unless all those rights belonging to Esau as the eldest son were given up to him. Esau, seeing he could not get food on any other terms, yielded, and gave up his birthright; and then his unloving brother allowed him to eat with him.

Years after this Jacob acted still more wickedly, not only to his brother Esau, but to his father also.

Isaac had grown old and blind; and not knowing how soon he might die, he desired Esau to go out hunting for venison, that he might eat of it, and then give him his last solemn blessing. But while Esau was away, Rebekah, who had heard what was said, bade Jacob fetch a tender kid from the flock, which she cooked to taste like venison; and then, dressing him in Esau's clothes, she told him to take it to his father, and pretend that he was Esau, in order that he might obtain the blessing designed for his brother. Jacob was afraid of being found out in this attempt to deceive his father; but at last he agreed to do as his mother had said; and when Isaac asked him who he was, he replied that he was Esau, and he begged his father to eat of the venison that he had taken for him. Isaac perceived that the voice was not that of Esau; but when Jacob assured him that he was really Esau, the poor blind old man believed him, and gave him the blessing which he had lied to obtain. It was a needless lie; for God had before ordained that Jacob should receive this blessing in place of Esau, and He would have brought it about in a righteous manner, had not Jacob sinned in order to gain it.

Presently afterward, Esau, who had really been for venison, brought it to his father, that he might receive his promised blessing. And then, to his great distress, Isaac discovered that his younger son had deceived him, and cunningly secured for himself that which had been intended for his elder brother.

Esau departs in anger.

Jacob's Dream

ESAU was so angry with Jacob for having twice supplanted him, first in taking away his birthright, and now in having deprived him of his father's blessing, that he threatened to kill him after Isaac's death; and Rebekah, fearing he would do so, sent Jacob away to her brother Laban at Padan-Aram.

Before he went thither Isaac confirmed to him the blessing he had already received; for, though Jacob had obtained it wickedly by deceit, his father knew that it was God's purpose that he should have it.

Noah and his sons worked to build the ark before the forty days and nights of rain should come to flood the earth (*Story on page 13*).

Abraham with Isaac, his son (*Story on page 24*).

Abraham prepares to sacrifice Isaac (*Story on page 25*).

The merchants to whom his brothers sold him took Joseph to the slave market (*Story on page 41*).

Isaac also desired him to take a wife of Laban's family, and then he sent him on his way.

While Jacob was on this journey, as he rested one night at a certain place, he had a wonderful dream. In it he saw a ladder set upon the earth, the top of which reached to heaven; and on this ladder the angels of God were ascending and descending. Above it stood the Lord God Himself, who spoke to Jacob, saying that He was the God of Abraham and Isaac, and that He would give the ground whereon he lay to him and to his children after him. He also told him that his descendants should be like the dust of the earth for number, and that in him all families of the earth should be blessed. And He promised to be with him, and to take care of him wherever he went, and that at last He would bring him back again to the land which He had given him.

Then, when Jacob awaked out of sleep, he knew that God Himself had been speaking with him. And he was afraid, exclaiming, "How dreadful is this place! Surely the Lord is here, and I knew it not."

In the morning he arose early, and, taking the stone on which his head had rested while he slept, he set it up for a pillar. And the name of the place, which was called Luz, he changed to Bethel, which means the "House of God."

And he made a solemn vow, that if God would indeed take care of him, and bring him safe back to his father's house, he would henceforth serve Him faithfully.

Jacob and Rachel

JACOB continued on his way, getting ever farther away from his brother Esau's wrath. At last he reached Haran, the place where his uncle Laban dwelt. He saw a green field, and in the field a well. Three flocks of sheep were lying there, resting, and waiting to be watered.

As Jacob drew near he greeted the shepherds and asked them whether they knew a man named Laban.

They replied, "We know Laban, and here, behold, Rachel, his daughter, cometh with the sheep."

As Rachel approached, looking sweet and beautiful, Jacob was deeply touched. He rolled away the stone which covered the well and watered the flock of Laban. Then he embraced his young cousin and lifted up his voice and wept.

When Rachel learned who Jacob was, she hastened to tell her father, Laban, and he greeted Jacob joyfully, and made him welcome in his home.

Jacob remained in Laban's home for a month, tending the flocks and herds. When Laban asked him what wages he wanted to receive, Jacob refused any money, but said, "I will serve thee seven years for Rachel thy younger daughter."

Jacob wished to have Rachel for his bride, for he had already begun to love her dearly. Laban thought this was a very good bargain, and readily agreed.

Jacob toiled for seven years in his uncle's service, and the time seemed to pass very quickly, for he knew that at the end of that time he would win the hand of Rachel, whom he loved more than ever.

A great wedding feast was prepared, and the wedding day came at last. Jacob was full of happiness, but, alas, Laban deceived Jacob, and forced him to marry Leah, the older daughter instead. Jacob was very angry at this, but Laban explained that a younger daughter cannot marry first, but would have to wait until the older daughter was married, so that Jacob would have to work for him seven more years if he also wanted to wed Rachel.

So Jacob, who had cheated his brother, was now cheated in turn.

Jacob worked for seven more weary years, always remembering, however, that at the end of this time he would win the hand of his beloved Rachel.

Finally, after seven more years had passed, Jacob also married Rachel, and now he was happy at last.

Jacob and Esau

JACOB remained twenty years with Laban, whose daughter Rachel he had married.

In those days men's chief riches consisted in flocks and herds; and Jacob had the care of those belonging to Laban. His uncle tried to deprive him of the wages which he had promised to give him; but, notwithstanding this, Jacob himself grew rich in cattle, and beasts of burden, and numerous servants.

At the end of the twenty years that Jacob had been with Laban, God bade him return to his own land; so he gathered together all his possessions, and set out on his way thither.

As Jacob still feared the anger of his brother Esau, whom he had so cruelly treated, he sent messengers before him into Edom, where Esau lived, to say that he, and all his family with him, were coming, and that he hoped his brother would be friendly with him. But when his messengers returned, bringing word that Esau, with four hundred men, was advancing to meet him, he was much afraid, thinking now his brother was going to kill him. So he divided his people and his flocks into two companies, that if the one were attacked, the other might escape away; and when he had done all that he could for self-defense, he prayed to God that Esau might not kill him, with his children and servants. Then he took a great number of his cattle, his sheep and camels, and sent them on before him in separate droves, bidding the men who were with them tell Esau, when they met him, that they were a present from his servant Jacob.

It was not long before Esau and his four hundred men came in sight; and then Jacob, putting his children in a place of safety, went forward to meet him, bowing himself down to the ground to do honor to his brother. But Esau, who had forgiven his brother's ill deeds, ran to him in the most loving manner, kissing him, and weeping for joy that they had at last met. And he asked him kindly about all the people with him, and what was the meaning of the droves of cattle he had seen on the road. Jacob told him that the people were his family, and that the cattle were for a present to himself. And when Esau refused to take it, he urged him, that he might be sure his brother had forgiven him. Then Esau returned to his own country, and Jacob, in time, came back to the land of Canaan, as God had promised that he should do.

Joseph Sold into Egypt

JACOB, whose name God had now changed to Israel, had twelve sons. Their names were Reuben, Simeon, Levi, Judah, Issachar, Zebulun, Gad, Asher, Dan, Naphtali, Joseph, and Benjamin. Of these, Joseph, the son of Rachel, was the one whom Jacob best loved. But his other sons, who were violent men, and had brought great sorrow upon him by their ill deeds, hated Joseph, and treated him unkindly; not only because he was his father's favorite, and had told him of their wrong doings, but on account of some dreams that he had had, which made them think he fancied himself superior to them all.

On one occasion, when Joseph was about seventeen years old, he dreamed that he was binding sheaves in the cornfields with his brothers, and that his sheaf stood upright, while all his brothers' sheaves bowed down to it. Another time he dreamed that the sun, and the moon, and eleven stars bowed down to him. And when he told these dreams to his father and brothers, they were all angry with him, asking him whether he expected that he should be the chief person in the family.

Joseph's father sent him one day to Shechem, where his brothers were feeding their flocks, to see if all was well with them. When they saw him coming, they said to one another, "See, here is this dreamer! Let us kill him, and throw him into a pit, and say that a wild beast has eaten him. Then we shall see what will become of his dreams."

But Reuben, his eldest brother, was not quite so wicked as the rest: he begged them not to kill Joseph, but to throw him into the pit alive; and he did it in order that, when the others were gone, he might rescue him, and send him back to his father. So they stripped off Joseph's many-colored coat, which his father had given him because he was his favorite, and threw him into the pit. But no sooner had they done this, than, seeing a company of merchants coming out of Gilead, on their way to Egypt, they determined to sell him to them for a slave. So they drew him out, and sold him for twenty pieces of silver. Then they were cruel enough to dip his coat in the blood of a kid that they killed, and to send it to their father, saying they had found it, and asking whether or not it was Joseph's coat. His father knew it at once; and, crying out that a wild beast had devoured Joseph, wept and tore his garments for sorrow, and refused to be comforted, because Joseph, his son, was dead.

Pharaoh's Dream

THE merchants who bought Joseph sold him to Potiphar, an officer of Pharaoh, king of Egypt, who treated him very favorably, and put all his affairs under Joseph's care. But after he had served his master faithfully for some time, Joseph was falsely accused of some wrong doing; and his master, without inquiring into the matter, shut him up in prison.

But God was with him in the prison, as He had been while Joseph was ruling over Potiphar's household; and He caused the keeper of the prison to put trust in him, so that he had the whole care of the other prisoners, and of all that was done there. Two of these prisoners, chief servants of Pharaoh, dreamed strange dreams, and God gave Joseph wisdom to interpret them. He told one of them that his dream signified that in three days he should be taken out of prison and hanged; the other prisoner's dream signified that in three days he should be released and restored to favor. And he begged this one, after he should be set at liberty, to try to get him also out of prison. But when the man got out of prison, he thought no more about Joseph for two whole years. At the end of that time, Pharaoh, to whose service he was restored, had two dreams that made him unhappy, and whose meaning none of his wise men could tell him.

He dreamed that seven fat cattle were feeding in a meadow, and that seven lean ones came and ate them up. Again he dreamed of seven ears of good corn on one stalk, and that seven blighted ones sprang up and devoured them. And when no one could tell him what these dreams meant, the chief butler remembered how Joseph had explained to him his dream in the prison. So he told the king, who immediately sent for Joseph out of prison, related his dreams to him, and asked him what they signified. Joseph answered the king that in these dreams God had showed him what He was about to do: that He was going to give Egypt seven years of plenty, and after them seven years of famine. And he advised Pharaoh to seek out some discreet person whom he might set over the land of Egypt, with officers under him, to store up, during the years of plenty, corn enough to supply them in the years of famine. Pharaoh thought the advice was good, and that no one was so fit as Joseph to do all this; so he made him ruler. And Joseph stored up the corn, so that, when the famine came, other countries sent to Egypt to buy food.

Joseph and His Brethren

THE land of Canaan, where Joseph's father and brothers were living, was one of the countries afflicted by famine; so, when they heard that there was corn in Egypt, Jacob sent his sons there to buy some. They did not know, and bowed down before him, that he was their brother whom they had sold for a slave. But Joseph knew them, and treated them roughly, telling them they were spies. They answered him that they were no spies, but honest men—twelve brothers, one of whom, Benjamin, the youngest, was with their father in Canaan; and another, Joseph, was dead. But he said that the only way of proving themselves honest men was for one of them to go and fetch their youngest brother, while he kept the others in Egypt. And, having said this, he put them all in prison for three days.

On the third day they were brought before Joseph again, and then he told them that one of them must be left in prison, while the others carried corn to their father, and brought back their youngest brother. When they heard this they were greatly distressed; and they said to each other that now

Joseph, the ruler of Egypt.

punishment was coming upon them for their cruelty, a long
time ago, to their brother Joseph.

Joseph wept when he heard his brothers speaking in this
way, for he understood what they said, though they did not
know it, as he spoke in a different language from theirs.
Then he sent them away with corn, keeping Simeon till
they returned with Benjamin. Jacob was very unwilling to
let him go; but their corn was soon done, there was none to
be had anywhere save in Egypt, and Joseph had said they

Joseph interviews his brothers.

should not have any more unless Benjamin were with them. So he was obliged to send him.

When his brothers came again, Joseph entertained them very kindly at first, but presently he made as though he would keep Benjamin for his slave. Upon this, Judah, who had promised to take care of Benjamin, pleaded so earnestly, offering to be a slave in his place, that Joseph told them he was their own brother whom they had sold into Egypt. And he forgave them. Then he sent for his father, and made them all live with him in the land of Egypt.

Moses in the Bulrushes

JOSEPH died in Egypt when he was a hundred and ten years old; and all the people mourned for him. Some time after this, when the descendants of Jacob had become very numerous, there was a king of Egypt who treated them in a harsh manner. He tried to make slaves of them, setting them to all kinds of hard labor. But, the more he oppressed them, the more they increased in number; and the Egyptians were afraid lest, in time of war, the Israelites might turn against them, and make their escape out of the land. So the king commanded that all the sons of the children of Israel, or Hebrews as they are also called, should be put to death as soon as they were born. But the Hebrews to whom he gave this wicked command did not obey him; at which the king was so angry that he ordered his own people to throw all these poor little children into the river.

At this time a Hebrew named Amram had a son born: he was a beautiful child, and for three months his mother, Jochebed, succeeded in saving him from the Egyptians. But at last she found she could no longer conceal him. So she

Moses a prince before Pharoah.

made an ark, that is, a sort of cradle, of bulrushes coated over
with pitch, laid him in it, and then placed the ark among the
reeds that grew by the riverside, while his sister stood watching in the distance to see what would become of him.

Presently the king's daughter, attended by her women,
came down to the river, and, perceiving the ark among the
reeds, she sent one of her servants to bring it to her. It was
accordingly brought; and when she saw the poor little child

crying, she was sorry for it, for she knew it must be one of the Hebrew children whom the king had commanded to be killed, and whose mother had laid it there, hoping that some one would have compassion on it. The child's sister, seeing how the princess pitied him, then came forward, and asked whether she should fetch a Hebrew woman to nurse it for her. The princess bade her do so. So she fetched his own mother, and the king's daughter told her to take the child away and nurse it for her. Then his mother joyfully carried her little one home again, and nursed him. When he was old enough to be taken to Pharaoh's daughter, she called him her son, named him Moses, which means "drawn out of the water," and had him taught all that was known to the Egyptians, who were a very learned people.

A PALESTINIAN SHEPHERD
WITH HIS SHEEP

THE STORY OF THE PICTURE
(on inside pages)

JACOB AND ESAU REUNITE
(Gen. 33: 1-20)

The previous night was one of suffering for Jacob. The fear and anxiety which confronted Jacob, in anticipation of meeting his estranged brother, has disappeared. They greet each other in warm affection. Esau, the warrior and man of the field, is supported by his soldiers and beasts of combat and burden. Jacob, on the other hand, has brought only the possessions of a shepherd, his family, and his flocks. They are symbols of his love for God and man which Esau willingly accepts and embraces.

COURT OF THE GENTILES, HEROD'S TEMPLE.

The Israelites' Burdens

MOSES was brought up in the court of Egypt. But when he was about forty years old, he went among his own people again, and was grieved to find how sadly they were oppressed by the Egyptians. Once he saw an Egyptian ill-treating a Hebrew; so he killed the man, and buried his body in the sand. The king would have put him to death for this, but Moses escaped into the land of Midian, and dwelt there.

One day, when he was feeding his flock near Horeb, God called to him out of a bush that flamed with fire, and yet was not burned. And He told Moses that He had seen the sufferings of the people of Israel, and would deliver them, and bring them into the good land of Canaan, as He had promised to Abraham. And He commanded him to tell Pharaoh to let the people go, that they might serve God in the wilderness. He also appointed various wonderful things to be wrought before Pharaoh, that he might know that He who had sent him this command was the true God, whom he and his people ought to worship.

Moses was very unwilling to go to Pharaoh, for he

thought the king would not heed what he said; but God would have him do it, and also told him to take his brother Aaron with him. So he went; and when he came before the king, Pharaoh asked who the Lord was that he should obey Him. And he told Moses and Aaron that they hindered the people in their work by telling them about their God wanting them to go and sacrifice to Him in the wilderness. It was only because they were idle that they wished to do so. They should not go. And he ordered that more work should be given them than before.

The Hebrews had been making bricks of clay mixed with straw. So Pharaoh commanded that no more straw should be given them, but that they should get it for themselves where they could; while, at the same time, they were obliged to make as much brick as when straw was found for them. But, instead of making bricks, their time was now spent in seeking straw; and they were beaten because the usual quantity of work was not done.

The poor Hebrews were very sad, and bitterly reproached Moses and Aaron for making their condition so much worse than it had been. And though God assured them, by Moses, that He would certainly deliver them out of Egypt, they were so unhappy and faint-hearted that they would not believe it.

Pharaoh's Overthrow

AFTER this, by God's command, Moses and Aaron went many times to Pharaoh to bid him let the people go. But Pharaoh would not, though God sent strange and terrible plagues upon him and his people to punish them for their wickedness, and make them obey Him. At length, as Pharaoh had commanded all the sons of the Hebrews to be slain, God in one night destroyed all the first-born in Egypt; and then, fearing for their own lives, the Egyptians hastily drove out the Israelites, men, women, children, and cattle, with their household goods, hurriedly gathered together. There were six hundred thousand men, besides women and children. God caused a pillar of cloud to go before them in the daytime, to show them the way they were to take, and at night He led them by a pillar of fire.

After the children of Israel had left Egypt, Pharaoh, though his kingdom had been nearly destroyed for his disobedience to God, was angry with himself for having let them go. So he gathered together a great army, and pursued them to where they were encamped, in the wilderness by the Red Sea. When the people saw they were pursued, they were much afraid, and reproached Moses for bringing them there; for they thought it would have been better to be slaves in Egypt, than to be killed in the wilderness. But Moses bade them not fear; God would deliver them. Then the pillar of cloud and of fire, that had gone before to guide them, removed, and went behind the camp, so that it stood between the Egyptians and the children of Israel. To the Egyptians it was cloud and darkness, so that they could not continue their pursuit; but to the Israelites it gave light.

Then Moses, as God had commanded him, stretched out his rod, or staff, over the sea; and the waters divided, standing like a wall on the right hand and on the left, leaving dry land between them, so that the whole multitude passed through the very middle of the sea to the opposite shore. The Egyptians, seeing this, hastened to follow; but God sent a violent storm upon them, which threw them all into confusion. And when they were in the middle of the sea, where the Israelites had gone safely, God bade Moses again stretch out his hand over it; and when he did so, the waters came back again to their place, and drowned Pharaoh, and all the Egyptians: there was not one of them left alive.

So God delivered the children of Israel, as He had said.

Moses Smites the Rock

AFTER the Egyptians had been all destroyed, the Israelites went forward into the wilderness; and when they had been traveling three days, they were in distress for want of water. They did indeed find some at a place called Marah, but it was so bitter they could not drink it. So again they reproached Moses, as they had done when the Egyptians pursued them to the Red Sea, asking him what they were to do for drink. Then God bade him throw into the water a certain tree which He showed to him; and when Moses had done this, it became quite good to drink.

In a few days after, the people were in want of food; and again they were angry with Moses and his brother Aaron, who was with him taking care of the Israelites. They said they wished they had stayed in Egypt, where they had enough to eat, for they had been brought into the wilderness only that they might die of hunger. Then Moses asked them why they murmured against him and Aaron, when it was God Himself who had brought them out of Egypt; their murmuring was really against God. And yet, though He was displeased at their conduct, He would supply them with food, that they might know that He was indeed their God. So, in the evening, great flocks of quail came about the camp for the Israelites to eat; and in the morning, when the dew was dried up from the ground, there lay upon it a small round thing, like coriander seeds. The people did not know what it was; but Moses told them that was bread that God had sent them. There it was, fresh every morning, except on the seventh day, which God had in the beginning made a day of rest. On that day He would not have them gather it, giving them twice as much on the sixth day, that they might have enough for the seventh. This was called "manna"; and when it was ground, like grain, they made bread of it. God gave it them for forty years, till they came to the land of Canaan.

But, though God had done so much for them, the children of Israel were a most ungrateful people. The very next time they wanted water, they were so angry with Moses that they were ready to kill him. Then Moses prayed to God to tell him what to do. And God bade him take some of the chiefs of the people, and go to a certain rock in Horeb, and strike it with his rod, and water should come out of it. So he took the men with him, and struck the rock, and water flowed abundantly.

Aaron's Golden Calf

WHILE the children of Israel were encamped in the wilderness, Moses' wife and his two sons, together with Jethro, his father-in-law, came to him there. And Jethro, seeing how Moses was overburdened with the care of so many people, advised him to appoint officers over them, under himself, who might attend to all their smaller concerns. But God Himself had the chief government of the people; and on Mount Sinai, where Moses spoke to Him and saw His great glory, He gave to them, not only the Ten Commandments, but many other laws and directions, for all they should do in worshiping Him.

That was an awful sight when God spoke to Moses on Sinai! For there were thunders, and lightnings, and a thick cloud, like the smoke of a furnace, about the mountain; and from out of it came a great voice of a trumpet, sounding louder and louder: and then Moses went up and spoke with the Lord God.

Moses was forty days in the mount, and the people began to wonder what had become of him. So they asked Aaron to make them some images which they might worship, and that might guide them out of the wilderness. Aaron knew there was only one God, yet he did as the people desired. He bade them bring their golden ornaments to him; and then he melted them, shaped the metal into the form of a calf (one of the false gods of the Egyptians), built an altar before it, on which the people might lay their offerings, and told them that was their god that had brought them out of the land of Egypt. The next day the people offered sacrifice to this calf, just as the heathen, who did not know God, worshiped their idols, or false gods.

But God saw this; and He was so displeased at their wickedness that He would have destroyed them all, had not Moses interceded for them. Then Moses came down from the mount to the camp, and asked Aaron how it was that he and the people had committed so great a sin. Aaron tried to excuse himself by laying the blame on the unruly Israelites. But there was no excuse for him. And after Moses had burned the calf, he ground it to powder, and threw it into the water that supplied the camp. God also, though he had granted Moses' prayer, commanded that great numbers of the people should be put to death for their sin.

The Ten Commandments

THE Ten Commandments which God gave on Mount Sinai were written by Himself on stone tablets. And when Moses came down from the mount, and saw the people worshiping the golden calf, in his anger he threw them down, and they were broken.

But after God, at Moses' prayer, had so far forgiven the sin of the Israelites as not to destroy them all, He bade Moses hew two tables of stone, like the first, and bring them to Him on Mount Sinai, that He might again give them His commandments. Moses did so, and went up early in the morning to the mount. He was in the mount with God forty days and nights, neither eating nor drinking; and when he came down with the stone tables, on which the Commandments had been again written, his face was so bright that the people could not look at him. He had to cover himself with a veil while he talked to them.

God had bidden him tell the people of Israel that if they kept His commandments, He would bless them, and make them prosperous; but if they did not keep them, He would give them into the power of their enemies, and afflict them

with all kinds of troubles. God also would have them prepare a place in which He might be worshiped; and, as the
people were traveling onward to the promised land, He bade
them make it like a tent, which might be carried along with
them, and set up when they rested on their march. This tent
was called the Tabernacle; and God gave exact directions
how it was to be made, and also how they were to make the
altar on which sacrifice was to be offered, and the ark, which
was a chest, to hold the tables of stone. The people were
glad to do what God desired them in this matter, and
brought such large quantities of precious materials to con-
struct the Tabernacle, and those other things that were to be
in it, that at last Moses was obliged to bid them bring no
more.

When all was completed, God commanded that the Tabernacle should be set up in the wilderness of Sinai. And
when it was set up, His glory filled it; a cloud also rested upon
it by day, and at night a light like fire. As long as God would
have the children of Israel remain in their camp in the wilderness, this cloud remained on the Tabernacle; when He
would have them go on their journey, the cloud was taken
up from it, and went before them. In this way the people
knew whether God would have them travel on, or stay where
they were.

The Return of the Spies

WHEN the children of Israel were encamped in the wilderness of Paran, Moses, by God's command, sent twelve men, one from each of the twelve tribes, or families into which they were divided, into the land of Canaan, that they might bring him word what sort of country it was, and what kind of people lived in it. He also told the men to bring back with them some of its fruits.

So the twelve men, who are called spies because they went to see the country, went, and were out forty days. When they returned, as it was the time when grapes were ripening, they brought with them, from Eshcol, a bunch of grapes, so large and ripe that two of them carried it between them. This, and other fruits that they had gathered, they showed to the Israelites, and told them that the country whence they came was very fertile, but that the people in it were so powerful and warlike that it would be impossible to drive them out, as God had said they should. They were giants, and lived in large cities, defended by walls. And though Caleb, a brave man, one of the spies, wished that the people should at once march forward and take it, the other spies repeated that it was impossible. Then the people began to reproach Moses and Aaron for bringing them into that wilderness to be slain by their enemies; and they threatened to put Moses away from them, and choose, in his place, a captain who might lead them back into Egypt. Caleb, and Joshua, another of the spies, entreated them not to rebel against God; for, if they obeyed Him, He would certainly, as He had promised, give them that rich country. But the multitude only clamored the more, and were even for stoning Moses and those with him. Then suddenly the glory of the Lord was seen in the Tabernacle; and God Himself, in His displeasure, declared that as the people would not believe Him, they should no longer be His people, nor have the good land He had promised them.

But Moses again prayed earnestly for the rebellious Israelites, begging God to pardon them. And God heard his prayer, and said that He would not entirely cast them off. But that none of those men, for whom He had done such great things, in delivering them out of Egypt, and feeding them in the wilderness, and who had yet constantly rebelled against Him, should enter into the promised land: they should all die in the wilderness. Only their children, together with Joshua and Caleb, should be brought into Canaan.

The Brazen Serpent

THE people were at first very sorry for having so displeased God. But they soon forgot it all; and the next time that they were without water in their encampment, they murmured, as usual, against Moses and Aaron.

Then God commanded Moses to take the rod with which he had struck the rock in Horeb, and before all the people to speak to a certain rock, which He pointed out, and it should give water for them and their cattle.

But now both Moses, and Aaron, who was to go with him, did wrong. They thought that speaking to the rock, as God had said, would not be sufficient; so Moses struck it twice with his rod, angrily asking the multitude whether he and Aaron must fetch them water out of the rock. And though, notwithstanding their disobedience, the water, when the rock was struck, flowed out in such abundance that all had enough, God told Moses and Aaron that because they had not obeyed Him when He bade them speak to it only, they should neither of them enter into the promised land. Aaron, whom God had appointed chief priest, died very soon afterward, on Mount Hor, and Eleazar, his son, was chosen by God as priest in his place.

The land of Edom, which God had given to Esau, now lay between the Israelites and the way by which they were to go to Canaan. So Moses sent messengers to the King of Edom, asking leave to pass through. But the king not only refused to let them pass through, but threatened to lead out his army against the Israelites; so they were obliged to turn aside, and go round Edom. There they met with so many difficulties that they got quite dispirited, and, as before, murmured against God.

Then God, to punish them, sent among them fiery serpents, which stung great numbers of the people, so that they died. The fear of death made the Israelites repent, and confess their sin in speaking against God. So they asked Moses to pray for them, that God would take away those dreadful serpents. And when Moses prayed, God told him to make an image in brass in the likeness of one of the serpents, and to set it up on a pole, and He promised that every one who was stung should be cured when he looked up to it.

Moses did as he was commanded. And every one who looked upon the brazen serpent was healed.

Balaam and the Ass

HE Israelites had to fight their way to the promised land, and God so often gave them victory in battle that the nations around were afraid of them.

Sihon, king of the Amorites, and Og, the king of Bashan, both came out with armies against them; but the Israelites overcame them, and took possession of their territories. The victorious army afterward pitched their tents in the plains of Moab; and Balak, king of that country, fearing he and his people should also be destroyed, sent to Balaam, who was a prophet (that is, one to whom God shows things that are going to happen), to come and pronounce a curse upon the Israelites, which might prevent their taking his kingdom from him. Balaam at first refused to curse the Israelites, for he knew that God had blessed them. But Balak entreated him, promising him honors and riches; and at last Balaam consented.

So, in the morning, he saddled his ass and went with them. But God was angry with him for desiring Balak's riches and honors, and sent an angel to stand in the way and oppose him. God, who can do whatever He will, enabled the ass, upon which Balaam rode, to see the angel; and she turned aside to avoid him. For this her master struck her. But again the angel stood before him in a path where there was a wall on each side; and the ass, seeing him, and trying to turn aside as before, crushed Balaam's foot against the wall. Then Balaam struck her again. But a little farther on the angel stood before them a third time; and the ass, seeing him, fell down under Balaam, who angrily struck her with his staff. God now wonderfully caused the ass to speak; and she asked Balaam why he had beaten her. Then God made Balaam himself see the angel standing with his drawn sword in his hand; and Balaam bowed down before him to the very ground. And the angel reproved Balaam for striking his ass, telling him that because he had wished to do what God did not will, God had sent His angel to oppose him in the way; and, had not the ass turned aside, he would have been slain. Balaam then confessed that he had done wrong, and offered to go back. The angel, however, bade him go on to Balak, but to be careful to speak only what God should bid him say.

So Balaam went on; and when he saw all the encampment of the children of Israel stretching far before him, by God's command he blessed the people whom Balak had sent for him to curse.

Pharaoh's daughter saw Moses in the bulrushes and asked his sister to find a nurse for him (*Story on page 48*).

God calls to Moses from the burning bush (*Story on page 49*).

Pharaoh's men attempt to cross the Red Sea (*Story on page 52*).

Samson carrying the gates of the city (*Story on page 73*).

Joshua at Jericho

THE children of Israel had now only to cross the River Jordan to enter the promised land of Canaan. Moses, for his sin at Meribah, or the waters of strife, where he struck the rock instead of speaking to it as he was told, had been forbidden to enter it with them. He was only allowed to see it at a distance, from the top of Mount Nebo. So, by God's command, he appointed Joshua to be their guide and leader into it. After Moses had done this, he died, a hundred and twenty years old.

Then God bade Joshua prepare to pass over the Jordan into the land He had promised to the Israelites. But, before they did so, Joshua sent two spies to the city of Jericho, which was fortified against them on the other side of the river. The people of the city were very much afraid of the Israelites, for they had heard what God had done for them from the time they left Egypt. So, when the King of Jericho sent men to take these spies prisoners, a woman of the city, in whose house they had lodged, hid them; and then begged, as her reward, that when the city should be taken, her life, and the lives of all her family, might be saved. The spies promised this; so then, as she lived on the town wall, she let them down by a cord through the window, and they returned to the camp.

When the people were about to pass over Jordan, the ark, in which were the two tables of stone, was carried before them by twelve priests; and, as soon as they entered the river, its waters were divided, and all the multitude went over on dry ground. Then they encamped at Gilgal, before Jericho; and there God commanded that the armed men of the Israelites, with the priests carrying the ark, should on seven days go round the city, with trumpets sounding; and He told them that on the seventh day the walls should fall down before them. So each day, for six days, as they had been bidden, they went once round the city; but on the seventh day they went round it seven times, as God had said; and at the seventh time, when the priests blew a loud blast with the trumpets, Joshua bade the people shout, for the city was theirs. Then they gave a great shout, and the walls of the city fell down flat before them, so that they marched straight into it, and burned it to the ground.

But Joshua remembered the woman Rahab, who had hidden the spies, and he brought her and her family in safety out of Jericho into the camp of the Israelites.

The Story of Gideon

THE children of Israel did evil in the sight of the Lord; and the Lord delivered them into the hand of Midian for seven years. The Israelites took refuge in dens and strongholds in the mountains, and in caves. At harvest time, when the crops which had been sown by the Israelites were ready for the reaping, the Midianites came with their numbers of camels and ate up the crops. They were in great numbers like grasshoppers, and when they left, the land was bare, with no food for man or beast.

The children of Israel cried out to God and wanted to know why this great trouble had come upon them, and He sent them a prophet to tell them that it was because He had brought them up out of Egypt, and had delivered them from all oppression, and He had told them not to worship the gods of the country in which they lived, for He was the Lord their God; but they had not obeyed Him, and for this they were being punished.

There was a man among the Israelites who did not want to worship any but Jehovah. His name was Gideon, and one day as he sat threshing wheat by the wine-press to hide it from the Midianites, an angel of the Lord appeared and spoke to him, saying, "The Lord is with you, mighty man of valour."

"I have chosen you to save Israel."

So the next day Gideon took ten of his servants and went up to the hill on which had been erected an altar to Baal and the Asherah, the false gods whom the people were worshiping. He threw down the false altars, and built an altar to God in the same place, and on it he made a burnt offering to God.

The next morning when the people saw what had been done, they cried out to one another.

"Who has done this thing?" they shouted.

Then the men of the city went to Joash, Gideon's father, and they asked him to send his son out, that he might be put to death.

Gideon's father refused, saying, "Why should you plead for Baal? If he is a god, he should plead for himself against the one who has wronged him."

Then all the Midianites and the Amalekites and the children of the east were gathered together, and went over, and pitched in the valley of Jezreel. The Spirit of the Lord came upon Gideon, and he blew a trumpet, and called a great army together. But before he sat out to save Israel, he wanted to be sure that he was the one chosen to do it, so he said to God: "If I am the one chosen to this task, I should like a sign. I will put this fleece of wool upon the earth. If the dew forms on the fleece, but not on the earth, I will know that it is indeed so."

And God did so that night. Then Gideon returned to his army, and prepared for the battle. But Jehovah said that his army was far too large, and he asked Gideon to send home all who were fearful and afraid. So twenty-two thousand went home, and ten thousand remained. But Jehovah said that it was still too large, and sent home all but three hundred.

That night Gideon went alone to the camp of the Midianites, and he heard one man telling of a strange dream.

"I dreamed," said the man, "and lo, a cake of barley bread tumbled into the host of Midian, and came to a tent, and smote it that it fell and overturned it, and the tent lay along."

And the other answered, "This is nothing else save the sword of Gideon, for into his hand hath God delivered Midian and all the host."

Gideon returned to his camp.

He called up his three hundred men, and gave each of them empty pitchers and lamps and trumpets. Then he led them to the enemy camp. When they came to the camp, the three companies blew with their trumpets, broke the pitchers, so that the lights shone out, and shouted, "The sword of Jehovah and of Gideon."

The Midianites were in utter confusion, and Gideon won an easy victory.

Jephthah's Daughter

T came to pass in time that the children of Ammon made war against Israel, and a man named Jephthah was made captain of the army.

Before he went forth to battle, he vowed a vow that he would offer up as a burnt offering to Jehovah the first thing that came to meet him from the doors of his house on his return home.

The Israelites were victorious, and Jephthah hurried home after the battle with joy in his heart. Alas! It changed soon to agony, for his little daughter came dancing forth to meet him. Jephthah tore his clothes and wailed, but his daughter understood and said quietly that he must do as he had vowed. She asked only to be allowed to go to the mountains with her companions for two months. After that she returned and quietly submitted to her fate.

Samson and the Lion

THE children of Israel made many other conquests after the fall of Jericho. On one occasion God caused both the sun and the moon to stand still in the heavens, that the day might be long enough for them to complete the defeat of their enemies. At length they had possession of almost the whole land of Canaan, and they divided it by lot among their twelve tribes, the descendants of Israel's twelve sons. Then God gave them rest from the attacks of their enemies round about them; and for a while they served Him faithfully.

But after the death of Joshua, and those who had come with him into the promised land, the people began to forget God, and to worship false gods. So, to punish them, God allowed their enemies to distress them on every hand. Yet, from time to time, He took pity upon them, and gave them rulers, called judges, under whom they were victorious in war. But, as soon as the judge was dead, they returned to their evil ways; and then God again let them fall under the power of their enemies.

The Philistines were the most powerful of the nations

that oppressed the Israelites; and to help them against these, God gave to them a judge named Samson.

Before he was born, an angel appeared to his mother and told her that her son should begin the deliverance of the people from the Philistines. She did not know it was really an angel, but told her husband that a man, who looked like an angel of God, had said these things to her. Then Manoah, her husband, prayed to God that the man might come again, and tell them how they should bring up their child. So God sent the angel again, and they still thought he was a man. But when they began to dress food for him, the angel bade them offer it to God as a burnt-offering; and when they did so, he went up, as it were, to heaven, in the flame that rose from the altar. Then they knew it was God's angel with whom they had been speaking.

When their child was born they called him Samson, and did all that the angel had said they should do with him. And God blessed Samson, and made him the strongest man that ever lived. One day, when he was going with his father and mother into the country of the Philistines, a lion sprang out roaring against him; and God suddenly gave him such strength that he seized it with his hands and tore it to pieces.

Samson and the Gates of Gaza

AMSON married the daughter of one of the Philistines; but afterward her father took her away from him, and, in revenge, he killed great numbers of them, and destroyed their crops and vineyards.

The Philistines then came out in great force against the men of Judah, and demanded that Samson should be given up to them. The men accordingly came to Samson, and said they must give him up to the enemy. So Samson let them bind him with strong cords, and take him to the Philistines. But at that moment God gave him strength to snap the cords asunder; and, snatching up the jaw-bone of an ass, he fell upon his enemies, and killed a thousand of them.

After this, Samson went to Gaza, a city of the Philistines, and at night the people shut him in, saying to each other that they would kill him in the morning. But in the middle of the night he got up, tore down the gates of the city, and, throwing them upon his shoulders, carried them to the top of a hill in the neighborhood. His enemies now saw that they could not overcome him by force, so they bribed a woman to get from him the secret of his strength. Samson deceived

Samson and the lion.

both her and them several times, but at last told her the truth, that if his hair were cut off, he should be no stronger than any other man. So, when he was asleep, she cut it off; and then, calling the Philistines, they took him, put out his eyes, and set him to grind corn. But as he toiled in prison, God gave his strength to him again. So one day, when the great men of the Philistines were going to worship their false god Dagon, and would have Samson make sport for them, he begged the boy who led him in to let him rest against the pillars of the building where they were assembled. Then, praying to God that He would once more enable him to destroy his enemies, he laid hold of the pillars, and, bending forward with all his might, pulled the building down, crushing both himself and thousands of the Philistines. Thus it happened that he killed more in his death than in life.

Naomi and Ruth

IN the days when the Judges ruled over Israel, there was a famine in the land. And a man named Elimelech, who lived at Bethlehem-Judah, together with his wife Naomi, and his two sons, Mahlon and Chilion, left their home on account of it, and went to live in the country of the Moabites.

While they were there Elimelech died, leaving Naomi and her sons, who married two women of the country, named Orpah and Ruth. In about ten years the sons died also; and then Naomi, hearing that the famine which had driven them from home had passed away, resolved to return thither with her daughters-in-law. But they had not gone far before Naomi, remembering that she was now poor, as well as a widow, thought it would be better for her daughters-in-law to stay among their own people than to go with her to what was to them a strange land. So she kissed them, and bade them return to their mother's house, praying God to bless them for their kindness to her and her sons. Her daughters wept, and refused to leave her; but she urged them to do so, till at last Orpah yielded, and, bidding Naomi a loving fare-

Naomi says goodbye to Ruth and Orpah.

well, went back to her own home in Moab. Ruth, however, still clung to her mother-in-law; and when Naomi would have had her follow her sister-in-law, who was gone to her own people and the gods of her country (for the Moabites were heathens, and worshiped the idol Baal), she answered her, "Entreat me not to leave thee, or to return from following after thee; for whither thou goest I will go, and where thou lodgest I will lodge: thy people shall be my people, and thy God my God. Where thou diest will I die, and there will I be buried: naught but death shall part thee and me." So, when Naomi saw how steadfastly Ruth loved her, she ceased urging her, and they went on together to Bethlehem-Judah.

When they arrived there all the people of the place were surprised to see them, asking, "Is not this Naomi?" But Naomi, full of sorrow for her dead husband and sons, and the poverty that had now fallen upon her, answered them, "Call me not Naomi (which signifies "Pleasant"), but Mara (that is, "Bitterness"), for the Almighty hath dealt very bitterly with me."

It was the time of barley-harvest when Naomi and Ruth returned to Bethlehem; and they were so very poor that Ruth went out into the fields to glean after the reapers.

One of the chief men of Bethlehem was named Boaz, a very rich man, who was a near relation to Elimelech, Naomi's husband. Ruth happened to go and glean in a field belonging to him; and Boaz, seeing her, asked the man who was over the reapers who she was. The man answered that she was Ruth the Moabitess, who had come to Bethlehem with her mother-in-law Naomi, and that she had asked him to let her glean in the field. Boaz then spoke kindly to Ruth, and bade her not to go to any other fields to glean; and he told her, when she was thirsty, to help herself to the drink that was brought to refresh his servants.

Ruth felt grateful to Boaz, and asked him how it was that he showed so much kindness to a stranger. He told her that he had heard how good a daughter she had been to Naomi; and that she had left her own father, and mother, and country, to come with her into a strange land. And he prayed that the God of Israel would bless and reward her. Then at meal-time he bade her eat and drink with the reapers. So she sat beside them; and Boaz himself set food before her. And when she returned to her gleaning, he desired the reapers to let fall some handfuls of grain on purpose for her, that she might gather the more.

When Ruth went home in the evening, she gave her mother-in-law some of her own dinner, which she had kept for her; and then she beat out the barley she had gleaned. There was so large a quantity of it that Naomi asked her where she had gleaned that day. Ruth answered, in the field of Boaz. Naomi was glad when she heard this; and, telling Ruth that he was their near kinsman, she said she must contrive to see the great man again, and make him understand that the poor gleaner was nearly related to him. So Ruth did as Naomi desired her. And when Boaz knew who she was, he blessed her, and said that he would do for her all that the law of the Israelites required from him as her nearest kinsman.

Then he called together the chief men of the city, and before them, as witnesses, bought back the piece of land that had belonged to Elimelech, and to which Ruth, as the widow of his son, was the next heir. After that he took Ruth for his wife; and their son Obed was the grandfather of David, who was afterward the great King of Israel.

Hannah Dedicates Samuel

FIFTEEN judges ruled the people of Israel during a period of four hundred and fifty years; that is, from the death of Joshua, till Saul was chosen as their first king. Samuel was the last of these judges; and he was a priest and a great prophet, as well as a ruler of the people. His father and mother were named Elkanah and Hannah. They were very good people, and year by year went up from the place where they lived to Shiloh, where the Tabernacle had been set up, to worship and offer sacrifice to God. This all the Israelites were obliged to do after they were settled in the promised land. Hannah had no children; and as she was grieved that she had none, she prayed to God, when worshiping at Shiloh, to give her a son, promising that if He would, she would dedicate him (that is, give him up) to the Lord God, in the service of the Tabernacle, from his childhood. God granted her request; and when the child was born she called him Samuel (which means "Asked of God"), because he had been given to her in answer to her prayer.

The first time after his birth that Elkanah and his family went up, as usual, to worship at Shiloh, Hannah did not go

TRADITIONAL SITE OF JESUS' BAPTISM
IN JORDAN.

THE STORY OF THE PICTURE
(on inside pages)

THE WALL IS FINISHED
(Neh. 4)

The great wall of Jerusalem is completely rebuilt. Nehemiah stands victoriously defiant upon the massive structure as flaming torches illuminate the scene below him. With Nehemiah are the loyal warriors and builders who fought and labored that the wall might be finished despite continuous enemy opposition. They now rest, amused at the reactions of their defeated enemies. The inspired leadership of Nehemiah has at last born fruit. He has brought confidence and security to his people and they rejoice in their success.

THE WELL ON THE ROAD
TO BETHLEHEM

with them. She told her husband she would not do so till Samuel was weaned, and then she would take him with her, and leave him with the priests, who might train him to serve God in the Tabernacle. Elkanah bade her do as she thought best in the matter. So when Samuel was weaned, she took him with her to Shiloh. And when she had offered sacrifice to God, she told Eli the high-priest, who was also at that time judge in Israel, that she was the woman whom some time before he had seen praying in the Temple (as the Tabernacle was also called), and that Samuel was the child she had prayed for. And now, as she had promised, she was come to give him to God, that he might be His priest.

Then, when Eli had given his blessing to Hannah and her husband, they returned home, leaving Samuel with him. And the child served in the ministry of the Temple, clad in a white linen garment that the priests wore. It was called an ephod. And every year that his mother came up to worship at Shiloh, she brought him a little coat, that she had herself made for him.

And as Samuel grew, God blessed him; and Eli, who was very old and nearly blind, was fond of this good little child whom everybody loved because he was good.

Samuel

THE high-priest Eli had two sons, named Hophni and Phinehas, who were both priests. But they were exceedingly wicked men; and when the people who came to worship complained to Eli of the wickedness of the young men, he reproved them so gently that they gave no heed to what he said. And God was displeased with him for not using his authority to make them do better.

One night, when Samuel was laid down to sleep, he heard a voice calling him; and thinking it was Eli, he got up and ran to him, to know what he wanted with him. But Eli bade him lie down again, for he had not called him. Again the voice called "Samuel," and again Samuel ran to Eli, who told him he had not called. But the third time that Samuel heard the voice, and ran to Eli thinking it was he, Eli became aware that it was God Himself who was calling to the child. So he bade him go and lie down again, and if the voice called him once more, to answer, "Speak, Lord, for thy servant heareth." Then, when he was laid down again, the voice called as before, "Samuel, Samuel." And when Samuel answered as Eli had bidden him, God told him that he was going to punish Eli and his sons in a fearful manner, because the sons had made themselves hated for their wickedness and profanity, and Eli had not prevented it as he ought to have done.

In the morning Samuel rose, and, as was his office, opened the doors of the Temple. But he did not tell Eli what God had said to him in the night: he was afraid of doing so, it was so very sad. . Eli, however, bade him come to him and tell him all. And when the poor old man knew that it was God's will to destroy him and his family, he would not murmur at it: he only said, "It is the Lord, let Him do what seemeth Him good."

Very soon after this the Israelites were fighting against the Philistines, and, thinking they should be sure of victory if the ark of God were with them, they fetched it into their camp from Shiloh. But for their sins God suffered them to be defeated; the ark was taken, and Hophni and Phinehas, together with thirty thousand of the Israelites, were slain. Poor old Eli meanwhile sat by the wayside, waiting for tidings of the battle. And when word was brought him that his sons were killed and the ark taken, he fell off his seat backward, and broke his neck.

Some time after Eli's death, Samuel judged Israel in his place.

David Anointed King

WHEN Samuel was very old, he made his sons judges, with himself, over Israel. But his sons took bribes, and did other things that they ought not to have done; and the people of Israel became so discontented, that they came to Samuel and desired him to give them a king in place of him and his sons. Samuel was grieved at this request; so he prayed to God to know what he should do. And God was displeased with the people for wishing to be governed by a king, like other nations, when He Himself was their king. Nevertheless, He gave them leave to have one, and told Samuel whom he should choose. This was Saul, the son of Kish, a man of the tribe of Benjamin.

So Samuel anointed Saul king over Israel as we have already seen; and when he was brought before them, all the people shouted, "God save the king!"

At first Saul was a good king, and did all that God commanded him. But he soon became disobedient; and as he persisted in ill-doing, God, who was patient with him for a while, at last determined that one more worthy than he should be chosen to be king after him, and whose children should succeed to the throne in place of Saul's children. So God bade Samuel take a horn of oil, and go to Jesse, an Israelite who lived at Bethlehem, and anoint one of his sons, whom He would point out to him, as the future king over Israel. Samuel was afraid of doing this, for he thought Saul, if he knew it, would put him to death. But God bade him go and offer a sacrifice at Bethlehem, and He would show him what to do.

So he went and called the chief men of the town, together with Jesse and his family, to the sacrifice. Then Jesse made his sons pass before Samuel, who, when he saw the eldest son, Eliab, a tall, fine-looking man, thought he must be the one whom God would choose to be anointed king. But God said He would not have Eliab; for He looked at the heart of man, not at his outward appearance. So seven of Jesse's sons, one after another, came before Samuel, and none of them did God choose. Then Samuel asked if all Jesse's children were there. Jesse answered he had one more son, David, the youngest, who was away keeping sheep. So David was sent for. He was a beautiful youth, with golden hair; and as soon as he came, God bade Samuel anoint him, for he was the one whom He had chosen.

So Samuel anointed him king. And the Spirit of God then came upon David, and remained with him from that day.

The Story of Saul

AUL was the son of Kish. He was tall and handsome and well-built, and from his shoulders upward, he was bigger than any of his people.

One day the asses of Kish strayed away and were lost; and Kish said to his son, "Take one of the servants with you and arise, go seek the asses."

They searched through Mount Ephraim, and through the land of Shalisha, but they did not find them. They passed through the land of Shalim, and through the land of the Benjamites, but still they could not find the asses.

Then Saul began to think of returning home, for they had been away for a long time, and he feared that his father would be anxious for their safety.

The servant suggested that they go to see a wise man who lived in a city near by and who had foretold many things which had come to pass. Together they went to the city to see the seer, and they met some maidens who told them that a sacrifice was being made that day and that the seer, whose name was Samuel, would be there to bless it; so they would be sure to find him.

Now, the Lord had told Samuel that he would send him a man from the land of Benjamin to be the captain and king of all the people of Israel. So when Saul appeared, Samuel pointed him out and said to the assembled people, "There is the man."

And to Samuel he said, "Come up with me to the high place. You shall eat with me today, and tomorrow I will let you go and you shall tell me everything that is in your heart. As for the asses, do not trouble about them, for they were found three days ago."

Saul was puzzled, for he could not understand the honor that was being bestowed upon him, but Samuel gave him no chance to protest. He took Saul and his servant to the feast, and gave Saul the choicest portion to eat. The next morning Samuel anointed Saul, and led him before all the people and proclaimed him the new king. Saul tried to hide, but as he stood head and shoulders above all the other people, it was an easy matter to single him out. Amid the shouts and cheers of the people he was made King of Israel.

David and Goliath

THE Israelites and the Philistines were now at war together, and the two armies were posted on two mountains, with a valley between them. And while they were drawn up in sight of each other, a giant, named Goliath of Gath, came out of the camp of the Philistines, and challenged any one of the Israelites to come and fight with him. If he killed the Israelite, then the Israelites were to yield to the Philistines; but if the Israelite killed him, then the Philistines would serve them. He was a huge giant, nine or ten feet high, clad from head to foot in heavy brazen armor. The staff of his spear was as thick as a weaver's beam. And for forty days this terrible giant came out, defying all the Israelites. Even Saul himself, the king, who was a brave man, was afraid of him.

Now at this time the three eldest sons of Jesse were in Saul's army; and their father bade David, who was tending his sheep at Bethlehem, go to the camp with some parched corn, and bread for his brothers. He arrived there just as the two armies were advancing to battle; and as he talked to his brothers, out came the giant, defying the Israelites, who fled at the very sight of him.

David was indignant at seeing the armies of God's chosen people so contemptuously treated by a heathen, and he asked those about him what should be done for the man who killed him. They told him that he should have honors and riches, and that he should marry the king's daughter. Then Saul, hearing what David had said, sent for him; and David told the king that he would go and fight the giant. Saul reminded him that he was but a youth, and the Philistine had been a soldier all his life. But David answered that he had killed a lion and a bear that had attacked his flock, and he knew that God would also help him to kill this great giant.

Then Saul would have given him armor and a sword, but David would not have them. He took only his staff and sling, with five smooth stones in his shepherd's bag, and went to meet the giant, who came on cursing and taunting him. But David, running forward, took a stone from his bag, and slang it at the giant, whom it struck in the forehead, so that he fell on his face to the ground, and David cut off his head with his own sword. Then the Philistines took to flight when they saw that the giant was dead.

David Playing Before Saul

WHEN Saul and David, and the whole army were coming home in triumph, after the defeat of the Philistines, the women of Israel, as they passed along, came out of all their cities to meet them with dances and songs of joy. And as they danced and played on instruments of music, they said, "Saul has slain his thousands, but David his ten thousands!" And Saul was so much displeased at their thus giving more honor to David than they did to their king, that from that day he began to regard him with jealousy and distrust.

From the time that he had so sinned against God as to cause Him to give the kingdom of Israel after his death to another, Saul had become liable to fits of sadness and severe gloom. God had withdrawn His Spirit from him, and he was miserable—almost mad. His servants, who were anxious to comfort him, thought that music would soothe the distressed mind of the king, and, as David played skillfully upon the harp, they would have him play before Saul. And, whenever he did so, Saul was refreshed, and became cheerful again. But after he had grown envious of David's renown, twice, when David was playing before him, he threw a spear at him to kill him. David, however, escaped unhurt.   Saul then tried in various ways to destroy him by means of his enemies the Philistines, setting him on duties that seemed as if they must cost him his life.   Still God preserved David alike from the Philistines, and from Saul's own servants, whom the wicked king had commanded to put him to death.   Then Jonathan, Saul's son, having sent David, whom he loved, to a place of safety, pleaded with his father for him, reminding Saul how faithful David had been to him, and what good service he had done the kingdom by killing the Philistine who had so frightened them all.   And Saul yielded to the pleading of his son, and promised that he would do David no harm.   So he was brought back, and served Saul as before.

War, however, soon broke out again between the Israelites and the Philistines, and David again defeated them with great slaughter.   This roused all Saul's ill-will against him; so that, when in one of his fits of gloom, David, as was his custom, was trying to cheer him with his harp, Saul rose and threw a spear at him with such force that, as David slipped aside, it stuck fast in the wall.   That night David made his escape, and never returned.

David and Jonathan

SAUL sent messengers hither and thither to take David, but they failed to find him. Jonathan meanwhile kept trying to save his friend; but when at last Saul threw his spear at him, in his anger at his continuing to plead for David, he perceived that all his efforts were useless. So he and David took leave of each other lovingly; the latter retiring to the wilderness, where he soon gathered together a band of followers.

While Saul continued his fierce pursuit of David, his life was twice in David's power, who refused to hurt Saul, though his followers urged him to kill the king.

On one of these occasions, David, to prove how easily he might have killed Saul if he would, cut off a piece of his robe when he was asleep. And then, when the king awoke, showing it to him, he besought him not to believe those who had told him that David desired to take his life. Saul's hard heart was softened by this appeal, and he said to David, "Thou art more righteous than I;" for David had returned him good for evil. Saul added that he knew David should be king after him; and he entreated that his sons might not be put to death when David came to the throne. David solemnly promised this, and then Saul returned from pursuing him. But David, not daring to trust himself with him, went back to his stronghold in En-gedi.

Saul's reconciliation with David did not last long. He was soon hunting him again with a force of three thousand men. He had pitched his camp in the wilderness; and David, with Abishai, one of his followers, came down to it at night. The people were all asleep, and Saul's tent was set up in the midst of the encampment. The two stole in among them, and came silently to the place where Saul lay sleeping, with his spear stuck into the ground by his pillow, surrounded by his guard, with Abner their captain, all fast asleep. Abishai wished to kill Saul, but David would not suffer him. Only to show Saul once more how completely he had been in his power, he carried the spear, and water-bottle, that stood by it, away with him to his own camp. When he got there he called out tauntingly to Abner, and the king's guard, asking whether they were not pretty defenders of their master, and bidding them send some one to fetch back the king's spear. Saul knew the voice; and when David complained to him of his merciless pursuit of one who had so often spared his life, he relented, and said he would do David no more harm.

David is King

SAUL, having been defeated and severely wounded in his last battle with the Philistines, killed himself for fear of falling alive into the hands of the enemy. After his death the tribe of Judah chose David for their king, and he reigned in Hebron between seven and eight years. At the end of that time he became king over the whole of Israel; and, having taken Jerusalem from the Jebusites, who had got possession of it, he made it his capital city, and lived there in a fine palace which he built for himself. He greatly desired also to build a temple, in which the ark of God might be placed, and in which God might be worshiped with more splendor than He had been in the Tabernacle. God was pleased that David desired to do this, but told him that not he, but his son Solomon, who was to succeed him, should build the Temple.

David had many children, and among these his son Absalom was his favorite. He was very beautiful, and not only his father, but all the people of Israel, loved him. But he was a vain, worthless young man, and caused his father much sorrow by his wicked conduct. He murdered one of his half-brothers; and then, when, after long banishment, he was permitted to come again into the king's presence, he very soon raised a rebellion against him, in order to seize the crown for himself; and such numbers of the people joined with him that David was obliged to make his escape from Jerusalem into the wilderness. The good king was sorely grieved that his own favorite son should seek his life; but he trusted that God, who had so often delivered him, would do so now. He soon drew round him forces enough to meet those of his rebellious son, and a pitched battle was fought between them in the wood of Ephraim. The troops of Absalom were defeated with great slaughter; and as he himself was flying from the field of battle, his mule carried him under a large oak-tree; his head caught between the branches, and the animal, galloping off, left him hanging there. One of David's army, who saw this, instead of releasing him, ran and told Joab, David's chief captain, who, though he had received a strict charge from the king to save the life of his son, hastened to him, and cruelly killed him by thrusting three darts through his very heart.

When word was brought to David that Absalom was slain, he wept and lamented for him, exclaiming, "Oh, my son Absalom, my son! would God I had died for thee!"

Solomon Crowned King

WHEN Absalom was dead, the people were eager to fetch the king home again; so eager, that they quarreled among themselves because the men of Judah, David's own tribe, were the first to bring him on his way to Jerusalem. And the quarrel ended in all the men of Israel again revolting from the king. Joab, however, who was a skillful soldier, though he was a very bad man, succeeded in putting down the insurrection.

But David's troubles were not yet at an end. First famine, and then pestilence, in which seventy thousand of the people died, afflicted his kingdom. And then, when he was old and feeble, apparently near death, his son Adonijah set himself up to be king, after his father, instead of Solomon, whom God had appointed to succeed David. By way of making his claim sure, Adonijah had taken upon himself royal state. Joab and other officers of the kingdom were with him, and the people acknowledged him as king.

News of this was brought to David, who at once determined to prevent disputes about the succession after his death by having Solomon crowned during his own lifetime.

David sets out (*Story on page 88*).

David was not afraid as he drew near Goliath, the huge giant of the
Philistines (*Story on page 89*).

Jonathan was Saul's son, and a firm friend of David. Even when Saul was jealous and angry at David, and would have taken his life, Jonathan made an agreement with David which saved his life (*Story on page 91*).

Elijah restoring the widow's son to his mother (*Story on page 104*).

So he called Nathan the priest, Zadok the prophet, and Benaiah the captain of his guard, and bade them, with a number of his officers, take Solomon, and, placing him upon the king's own mule (which it was death for any subject to ride), bring him down to Gihon, a fountain near Jerusalem, and there, with sound of trumpet, anoint, and proclaim him king over Israel. So they took him thither, and proclaimed him king; multitudes following and shouting, "God save King Solomon!" till the city rang again.

Adonijah and his friends were at this time rejoicing together; and while they were yet feasting, in came one of their party to tell them that David had actually made Solomon king of Israel. When they heard this, they were so frightened that each one stole away as quietly as he could. And Adonijah, fearing that his life might be forfeited for attempting to seize the kingdom, fled to the altar for protection; for he who laid hold of the horns of the altar was considered under God's protection, and therefore safe from his enemies.

But Solomon sent for him, promising him safety if he submitted to him. So Adonijah came, and did homage to his brother, who let him go home peaceably.

Soon after this David died, and was buried at Jerusalem.

The Judgment of Solomon

SOLOMON was the greatest king that ever reigned in Israel; he was also one of the wisest men that ever lived. When he first came to the throne, God appeared to him one night in a dream, and asked what gift He should bestow upon him. Solomon prayed that He would give him wisdom to govern his people. God was pleased that he had asked wisdom instead of riches, or conquests, or long life, and He told Solomon that because he had done so, not only would He make him wiser than any man who ever lived, but that he should be rich and famous above all kings of the earth. And if he would obey Him in all things, long life should also be added to the other good gifts which were to be his.

In those days it was the custom for kings to sit in some public place, where such of their subjects as had wrongs to complain of might plead their cause before them, and obtain justice. One day two women came before Solomon. One of them told him that she and the other woman both lived in one house, and each had a very young child; that in the night the child belonging to the other woman died, and its mother exchanged it for the living one, putting her own dead child in her neighbor's bed as she lay sleeping, and taking the living child to herself. In the morning, the mother of the living child found out the cheat; but she whose child was dead would not give up the one that she had stolen, for she said it was her own. And the two women stood there before the king, each one contending that the living child was hers, and that the dead child belonged to the other. Then Solomon desired his people to bring him a sword; and when it was brought, he bade them divide the living child in two, and give half of him to each of the women. The woman who had falsely claimed the child made no objection to this decision. But the real mother could not bear it. Rather than have her son killed, she was willing to lose him altogether; and she cried out in an agony, "O my lord, give her the living child, and in no wise slay it!" Then the king saw at once to which of them the child belonged; and he said, "Give her the living child, for she is its mother."

And all the people of Israel, when they heard of this judgment of Solomon, knew that God had indeed given him wisdom to do justice among his subjects; and they held him in great awe and reverence.

The Queen of Sheba's Visit to Solomon

SOLOMON had vast treasures of gold and silver, and precious things of every kind. His people also were rich and happy. Solomon worshiped and served God faithfully; and God, as He had promised, blessed him greatly.

When David had desired to build a house, or temple, for God's worship at Jerusalem, God had told him that his son Solomon should build it. So, when he came to the throne, Solomon built this temple of the richest materials, and in the most costly manner. Hewn stone, cedar, olive-tree wood, fine brass, pure gold, silver, and precious stones, were there in abundance; and artificers from Tyre, who were famous for their skill, wrought them for him. The Temple, which was placed on Mount Moriah, was seven years in building. When it was finished, Solomon dedicated it to God in a solemn assembly of the people; and the Lord God filled it with His glory, as He had done the Tabernacle in the wilderness.

The wisdom of Solomon was celebrated not only among his own people, but in all parts of the East, whose kings sent messengers to him, that they might hear it for themselves.

The Queen of Sheba came herself to Jerusalem, with a great train of people, and camels carrying gold, precious stones, and spices, as presents for the great king, that she might know, by conversing with Solomon, whether he was so wise as had been told her. And when she heard his wisdom, and had seen the splendor of his court and palace, she was so overpowered that she fainted. And she said to the king that before she came she did not believe what had been told her in her own land of his wisdom and greatness, but now she saw that not even the half of it had been made known to her. Happy were they who served before him, and continually heard his wisdom. And she gave thanks to God for having given such a king to His people Israel. Then, when Solomon had also given her costly presents, she and her train returned to their own country.

But as Solomon grew older, instead of serving and worshiping God as he had done, he began to worship false gods. And then God, as He had threatened, let trouble come upon him and his kingdom, so that, after his death, ten of the tribes were taken away from his son, and set up into a separate kingdom, that of Israel, which was never again united to the kingdom of Judah.

Elijah Fed by Ravens

VERY soon after the separation of the twelve tribes the kingdom of Israel fell into idolatry. Jeroboam, its first king, set up golden calves in Dan and Bethel, the two extremities of his dominions, to prevent his people going up to Jerusalem (which belonged to the kingdom of Judah) to worship God. But, though they worshiped these images, they had not entirely rejected the true God. It was under Ahab, the sixth king, a weak and wicked man, whose wife, Jezebel, was even worse than himself, that the worship of the true God was put down, and that of Baal established in its place.

God was angry both with Ahab and his people for their idolatry and persecution of His priests, who were put to death in great numbers; and, as a punishment for these sins, He sent Elijah to tell Ahab that for three years and a half neither dew nor rain should fall in the land of Israel. As soon as Elijah had foretold this great evil, God bade him hide himself from the rage of Ahab in a certain place near the brook Cherith, where He had commanded the ravens to feed him. So he went and dwelt by the brook, which afforded him water to drink, while the ravens, as God had said, brought him food morning and evening. But, as no rain had fallen, in time the brook dried up, and then God bade him leave his present hiding-place, and go to Zarephath, near Sidon; for He had commanded a widow, who lived there, to provide for him. Elijah immediately went to Zarephath; and when he came to the gate of the city, he saw the woman gathering sticks. He called to her, and asked her to give him some water to drink; and as she was going for it, he begged her also to bring him a morsel of bread. The poor woman turned round, and told him she had no bread. All that she had was a handful of meal in a barrel, and a little oil in a bottle, and she had just been gathering wood to cook it for herself and her son; after they had eaten it, they must lie down to die, for she knew not where to get more. Elijah bade her do as she had said, but to make him a little cake first, and afterward for herself; for God, he assured her, would cause her meal and oil to last till the famine should be at an end. So the woman made him the little cake first; and he, and she, with her family, were fed out of the handful of meal and vessel of oil for many days. Neither of them failed till the day when God sent rain upon the earth, and so took away the famine.

Elijah Restores the Widow's Son

WHILE Elijah was with the widow of Zarephath, her son fell ill and died. His mother feared it was for some sin of hers that her child was taken from her, and that it was the prophet who had caused his illness. In her distress, she said this to Elijah reproachfully. But he only bade her bring her son to him; and then, lying down with the child on his own bed, he prayed earnestly that God would let its soul come into it again. God heard his prayer, and brought the child to life again; and Elijah carried him down to his mother.

When the three years and six months were past, God bade Elijah go again to Ahab, for He was now about to send rain upon the earth. At this time Ahab, and Obadiah, the governor of his household, a man who worshiped God, had gone in different directions to seek grass for the king's horses and mules. As Obadiah went on his way, Elijah met him, and bade him tell his master where he might find Elijah; for Ahab, thinking it was he that had brought famine upon the kingdom, had angrily sought him in all countries. Obadiah was unwilling to carry Elijah's message, for he feared that as soon as he had left him, God might command him to go to some other place, and then, when Ahab came and found no prophet there, he himself might be put to death for having misled the king. But Elijah replied that he would assuredly show himself to Ahab that day; and then Obadiah went to tell him.

When Ahab met Elijah, he haughtily asked whether he were not the man that troubled Israel. But Elijah answered that it was not he, but Ahab and his family that had brought affliction upon the nation by their wickedness. And he desired that the king would gather together all the priests of Baal on Mount Carmel, where he would offer sacrifice to God, and they to Baal; and the god whose sacrifice was consumed by fire from heaven should be acknowledged to be the true God. Ahab did this. The priests of Baal built their altar, and from morning to evening kept crying, "O Baal, hear us!" But there was no answer; their false god could do nothing for them. Then Elijah prepared his sacrifice; and when he called upon the Lord God, fire came down from heaven, that burnt up the sacrifice, and the wood, and even the stones of the altar. And then all the people bowed to the earth, exclaiming, "The Lord He is the God! The Lord He is the God!"

Elijah Taken to Heaven

ELIJAH returned with Ahab to Jezreel, a beautiful place where the king had a palace. But Jezebel threatened to kill the prophet; so he fled for his life out of Israel, into the kingdom of Judah, to Beersheba. There he left his servant, while he himself went a day's journey into the wilderness. Here, weary and worn out with his troubles, he lay down to sleep under a juniper-tree, and begged God to let him die. But while he slept, an angel touched him, bidding him rise and eat; and when he looked, he saw a cake baked on the coals, and a bottle of water by his side. So he ate and drank, and then lay down again. A second time the angel touched him, and bade him rise and eat; and that food which God had sent him sustained him for forty days and nights, while he traveled through the wilderness to Mount Horeb. And there, after storm, and earthquake, and fire, God appeared to him in a wonderful manner.

At length the time came when God would take Elijah to heaven without dying like other men. And as he and Elisha, who was to succeed him as prophet, went on their way from Gilgal to the River Jordan, Elijah, knowing what God was about to do for him, tried to persuade Elisha to leave him to go on alone. But Elisha clung lovingly to his master, and would not leave him. Then, at Bethel and Jericho, scholars of the prophets, who lived there, came out to them, asking Elisha if he knew that God would that day take away his master from him. Elisha answered them, "Yea, I know it;" and again Elijah would have sent him away, but he would not go. So they traveled together till they reached the river, where Elijah wrapped his mantle together, struck the waters, and they were divided, standing on each hand, so that he and Elisha passed over on dry ground. And as they still went on, suddenly there appeared in the air a chariot of fire, with horses of fire, which, parting the two asunder, carried up Elijah in a whirlwind to heaven. And when Elisha saw it, he cried after him, "My father, my father, the chariots of Israel, and the horsemen thereof!" Then he took the mantle that fell from Elijah as he went up, and turned back to the Jordan; and as he stood on its bank, he struck the waters, exclaiming, "Where is the Lord God of Elijah?" Then the waters were divided as they had been before, and Elisha went over on dry land.

Elisha's Death

HEN the young men who were in the schools of the prophets saw Elisha divide the waters of Jordan, they knew that God was with him, as He had been with Elijah; and they came and bowed down to the ground before him, to do him honor. They, as well as Elisha, had seen Elijah taken up by the fiery chariot; but they thought that God might perhaps have carried him, in that way, to some other part of the country. So they begged Elisha to let fifty of them go and seek him. Elisha at first forbade their doing so, but at last he gave them leave. So they sought Elijah for three days. But they did not find him, for he was with God in heaven.

Then the people of Jericho came to Elisha, complaining that, though the situation of their city was beautiful, as he saw, the water was almost poisonous, and the soil was barren. So he told them to bring him a new cruse, or bottle, with a little salt in it. And when it was brought, he went to the spring whence the water that supplied the neighborhood rose, and throwing the salt into it, he declared that God had taken away the unwholesomeness of the water, so that from that time neither men nor cattle should be injured by drinking it; nor should it any longer render the soil unproductive, as it had done.

After this, Elisha went to Bethel; and when he was near the city, some young men came out ridiculing and insulting him; and they mockingly bade him "go up," as his master had done. This was a shocking sin, for it was turning into jest that great miracle that God had just done, of carrying Elijah, living as he was, into heaven. Elisha knew that God's anger would fall upon them for such wickedness; and, turning back toward the young men, he told them that they would be punished. And immediately two fierce she-bears rushed out of the wood, and killed forty-two of them.

God enabled Elisha to do many miracles. He brought a dead child to life again. He healed the Syrian general, Naaman, of an incurable disease; fed a hundred of the prophets with a small quantity of bread; and did many other wonderful works.

When Elisha lay dying, Jehoash, king of Israel, came, and wept over him. Then Elisha bade the king shoot an arrow out of the window, and afterward strike the ground with the whole quiver-full, to show the king that he should overcome his enemies, the Syrians.

When he had done this, Elisha died.

Jehoash the Boy King

WHEN Jehoshaphat died, his eldest son Jehoram became king in Judah in his place. His wife was Athaliah, the daughter of Ahab and Jezebel, and together they did a great many wicked things.

Jehoram slew all his brothers in order to get the riches which his father had left to them. He built places in the mountains of Judah and in Jerusalem for the worship of Baal. When he died, after ruling for eight years, his son, Ahaziah, became the ruler. He, too, was very bad, and his rule was a short one. When he was killed, his mother saw that no one was left to take over the throne; so she planned to be the ruler herself. Of course, Ahaziah had some children, who were her grandsons, and she had other grandchildren too, but she decided that they must all be killed so that she could be made queen.

Only one of the grandchildren escaped—a tiny baby named Jehoash. He was hidden away by his father's sister, and he was kept hidden for years, in a set of chambers built round the Temple.

Athaliah became the queen, and since she was so willful and powerful, even those who did not approve of her had to pretend that they did. She established the worship of Baal again, and even took some of the Temple treasures and placed them in the House of Baal.

Jehoash remained hidden in the temple for six years, and he was taught all about Jehovah and the laws of Jehovah by his aunt and her husband, who was the High Priest of the Temple. (That was why the child could remain hidden in the Temple chambers for so long.) Finally the wickedness of the queen and her court became so great that the High Priest of the Temple decided that the only way to save the entire nation from destruction would be to place the young prince on the throne.

So after he had made his plans carefully, the Priest of Jehovah called the Guardsmen and soldiers of the temple together. He gave them weapons which had been hidden by David in the Temple. Then he brought forth Jehoash from his hiding place, and the assembled gathering proclaimed him king.

Of course Athaliah was very angry when she learned what had happened, but it was too late. She was driven out of the Temple; and as she was trying to escape, she was killed in the excitement.

As long as the Priest of the Temple, Jehoiada, was alive, Jehoash was a good king. He restored the Temple, which had fallen into bad repair through long neglect, and he brought the people back to the worship of Jehovah.

Jehoash was seven years old when he became king, and he reigned for forty years in Jerusalem.

The Story of Esther

AHASUERUS was a rich, powerful king. Once he held a feast which lasted for several days. At the end of the feast, he sent seven ministers to Vashti, his queen, of whose beauty he was very proud. He asked her to come and stand before all the people so that they might all see her great beauty and fairness. Vashti refused to come, and Ahasuerus was very angry. He sent his wise men to tell her that she was no longer queen, for she was a very bad example to other wives. His wise men advised him to choose another queen.

After some search, he chose a young girl named Esther. Her father and mother were dead, and she had been brought up by her cousin, a Jew named Mordecai. He loved her as his daughter, and he made her promise not to tell the king that a Jew was her cousin.

One day Mordecai was sitting in the gate when he heard two wicked men planning to kill the king. He contrived to meet Esther and tell her, and she warned the king. The wicked men were killed, and a note was made in the king's record book that Mordecai the Jew had saved his life.

FISHERMEN MENDING NETS BY SEA
OF GALILEE

THE STORY OF THE PICTURE
(on inside pages)

SHADRACH, MESHACH, AND ABEDNEGO
(Dan. 3)

Shadrach, Meshach, and Abednego have just stepped out unharmed from the fire of the roaring furnace. Not a hair is singed, their clothing is not scorched, and there is not even the smell of fire about them. They stand calmly before the awestruck king and his attendants. Although the fire could not touch the three boys, the king's soldiers who had thrust Shadrach, Meshach, and Abednego into the great furnace, now lie prostrate in death—killed instantly by the searing heat of the intense fire.

Nebuchadnezzar and his followers shield their faces from the blinding light and burning heat of the soaring flames as obedient servants come forward with food and drink for the faithful three. The king is now about to honor and proclaim the God of Israel as Almighty and alone deserving of worship.

A TYPICAL SCENE OF WILDERNESS
IN PALESTINE.

Now, it happened that one of the king's chief advisers, a man named Haman, was an enemy of Mordecai. Haman wanted everyone to bow to him, but Mordecai refused to do it; and Haman decided to punish him, and other Jews, whom he hated, as well.

One day Haman went to the king with a story that a certain people in the country would not obey the king's laws. Ahasuerus believed the story and ordered Haman to punish them, and he gave him a ring as a sign of his authority. So it was ordered that all the Jews in the country be killed, men, women, and even tiny children. Mordecai sat outside the palace gates in sackcloth and ashes and wept. Esther's maids came to tell her about it. She sent for him, but he did not come to see her, only sent her a letter telling her what was to happen and asking her to use her influence with the king to save their lives.

Esther dressed in her most beautiful robes, and then she went in to see the king, although in fear and trembling, for she was not to go to him unless he sent for her. However, when he saw her he was not angry, but asked her what she wanted.

"It shall be given to you, even though it be half of my kingdom," he said.

Esther said that she only wanted him to come to a feast she was preparing, and she wanted Haman to come too. Haman was prouder than ever, and so angry that Mordecai did not bow to him as he went through the palace gates, that he had a gallows built and resolved to ask the king's permission to hang Mordecai before the banquet.

The king was wakeful that night. He ordered his servants to bring the book of records, and by chance they came upon the part telling how Mordecai had saved the king's life.

"And how have we rewarded him?" asked the king.

When he found out that nothing had been done, he called to Haman and said, "What shall be done for a man whom I would like to honor?"

Of course Haman thought that the king meant to honor him. So he said, "Let the robes you used to wear be put on him, and let your crown be put upon his head. Have him escorted through the city by one of your princes, and tell everyone that this is a man whom you wish to honor."

Imagine his disappointment when he found out that it was Mordecai the Jew to whom the honor was being done.

At the feast, the king asked Esther what she would like to have, and she said, "Please save the lives of my people. It is ordered that all the Jews shall die, and since I am one of the Jews, I must die too."

When the king learned that Haman had ordered the death of the Jews, he was so angry that he ordered Haman hanged on the very gallows he had built for Mordecai.

Job and His Three Friends

IN the land of Uz, a country of Arabia, lived a man named Job. He was one of the greatest and richest men in that country; he had sheep, camels, oxen to cultivate his land, and asses, and servants, almost without number. He was also a very good man; he worshiped and obeyed God, and did no wrong to any one. But God thought fit to send him great losses and afflictions, to see whether, when he was poor and miserable, Job would still love and serve Him.

One day a man came in haste to Job, telling him that as his oxen were plowing, a company of armed robbers had fallen upon them, killed all the plowmen and herdsmen but himself, and had then carried off the cattle. While this man was speaking, in came another, saying that lightning had burned up all the sheep, and the shepherds with them. Before this one had done came yet another messenger, bringing word that robbers had seized Job's camels, and killed the servants that were with them. And then a fourth rushed in, with worse news than all the rest; for a violent storm had arisen, which, catching the house where Job's children were assembled, had blown it down, crushing them all in the ruins. Then Job rent his garments for very grief, but he did not murmur against God. He said, "The Lord gave, and the Lord hath taken away; blessed be the name of the Lord!"

But the next thing was that Job himself was seized with a most painful and loathsome disease, while his wife, instead of comforting him, cruelly taunted him with his patience under such sore evils, wickedly bidding him "curse God and die!" Yet then he only said, "Shall we receive good at the hand of God, and shall we not receive evil?" Then three of his friends came to him, and, weeping over his sad condition, sat silent upon the ground with him. But, though they were very sorry for him, they unjustly thought that his sufferings were in punishment for some wickedness that he had done. And when Job knew this, his wonderful patience failed him for a time, and he broke out in bitter lamentations and complaints of their cruelty. Yet he forgave them, and prayed God to forgive what they had said amiss about Him.

But Job was not quite faultless, as he had imagined. And when he confessed this to God, his trial came to an end; and God gave him back, not only all that he had lost, but twice as much as he had before.

Isaiah

IN Judah there was a prophet named Isaiah, who predicted the coming of Christ, and who warned the people to repent before His coming. He prophesied that Syria and Israel would be subdued by Assyria. And he prophesied many other things which came to pass. He wrote a great part of the book of "Isaiah" and in it he tells the people:

"Wash you, make yourselves clean. Put away the evil of your doings. Cease to do evil. Learn to do well. Seek judgment, do justice to the oppressed; judge the fatherless, plead for the widow."

Hezekiah was the son of David, the ruler of Judah, and one day he became very ill. Isaiah came to visit him, and he said: "Thus saith the Lord, 'Set your house in order, for you shall die, and not live.'"

Hezekiah turned his face toward the wall and prayed to the Lord, and he wept sore.

Then the Lord spoke to Isaiah and told him to go back to Hezekiah and tell him that He had seen Isaiah's tears and heard his prayers, and that he would add fifteen years to his life.

Now, at this time Jerusalem was in danger from the king of Assyria, and Jehovah told Isaiah that He would deliver the city out of the hand of the king of Assyria.

And as a sign that He would do all this, he would turn the shadow of the sundial backwards ten degrees.

Isaiah told Hezekiah to take a lump of figs and put it on the boil which was making Hezekiah so ill; and soon he was completely recovered.

Then Hezekiah made a song of thanksgiving, for Jehovah had saved him; and he wanted to sing his songs to the stringed instruments all the days of his life.

As for Isaiah, he continued to go about and prophesy the new Jerusalem.

Jeremiah Weeping over Jerusalem

THE people, both of Israel and Judah, fell into every kind of wickedness; and though God's prophets often reproved them, they continued in their sin. So at length God punished them by letting their enemies entirely overpower them, and carry them away captive to other countries.

The Assyrians destroyed the kingdom of Israel; and in about one hundred years after, Nebuchadnezzar, king of Babylon, put an end to that of Judah.

Jeremiah was one of the last prophets who tried to save the people of Judah from the punishment that was coming upon them for their sins. He was very young when he first began to warn them of their danger; and at that time a very good king, named Josiah, reigned in Judah, who did all that he could to turn his people from the worship of their false gods. But they were little, if any, the better for either his laws or Jeremiah's teaching; and when the king died, they began to ill-treat the prophet for his endeavors to do them good. They imprisoned him, put him in the stocks, and even threatened to kill him. At last God's judgments really came upon them. The Chaldeans, under Nebuchadnezzar their king, laid siege to Jerusalem. At first they were driven back; and then the people thought Jeremiah had not spoken the truth when he said that they should be carried prisoners to Babylon. But Jeremiah assured them that it would certainly be so in the end, and that they should remain captives in Babylon seventy years, after which God would bring them back to their own land.

Then some of the chief men of the city went to Zedekiah, the king, and begged him to put Jeremiah to death for disheartening the people. Zedekiah bade them do what they would with Jeremiah; so these men took him and threw him into a deep, filthy dungeon, where they left him to die of hunger. But when one of the king's officers heard what they had done, he went in haste to the king, and told him how cruelly Jeremiah had been treated. Then the king commanded him to bring up Jeremiah out of the dungeon. So the officer went to the dungeon and drew him up.

When the city was taken by Nebuchadnezzar, he gave Jeremiah leave either to go with him to Babylon, or to stay among his countrymen. Jeremiah chose to remain with his own people, weeping, and lamenting sore over the destruction of the Holy City.

Ezekiel

EZEKIEL was another of the prophets. He lived in the land of the Chaldeans by the river Chebar. One day a vision came to him. Ezekiel fell upon his face, as he heard the voice of the Lord speaking to him.

"Son of man, stand upon your feet," said the voice.

Ezekiel managed to stand up, and so he heard the commands of the Lord. The voice directed him to go to the children of Israel, for they were sinful and rebellious against the Lord. Ezekiel was to speak the Lord's words to them, and he was not to be afraid of them nor dismayed by their looks.

Then the voice commanded him to eat what he would find in his hand. It was a roll of a book, and Ezekiel ate it. He said that it was sweet as honey in his mouth.

Then the spirit lifted Ezekiel up, he heard a sound of rushing wings, and a noise of wheels which he had heard before. He was taken to Tel-abib, where the captives were.

After that Ezekiel went about among the children of Israel, and in stories and parables and exhortations, he warned them of things to come, and of the sorrowful consequences of their deeds.

Nebuchadnezzar's Dream

N the second year of the reign of Nebuchadnezzar, he had dreams so that his spirit was troubled and he awakened from his sleep.

He called his magicians, and his astrologers, and his sorcerers to see whether they could learn the meaning of his dreams. They all came and stood before him, and he said, "I have dreamed a certain dream, and my spirit is troubled to know the meaning of this dream."

The Chaldean sorcerers said, "Oh, king, tell us the dream, and we will tell you the meaning of it."

The king answered and said, "The dream has gone from me. But you must tell me the dream and the meaning of it, or you shall be cut into pieces and your houses shall be destroyed. But if you tell me the dream, you shall receive gifts and honors and great rewards from me."

Again they begged him to tell them the dream, but the king answered angrily that they were only trying to gain time.

The sorcerers were frightened and said that there was no one on earth who would tell the king what he desired.

The king was very angry and ordered all the wise men to

be put to death. Daniel had not been at the meeting, but the king's officers sought him out to kill him. He wanted to know the reason, and went bravely before Nebuchadnezzar and promised that if the king would give him time, he would show the interpretation.

Daniel and his three companions went home and prayed to the God of Heaven; and that night, in a vision, the secret was revealed to Daniel. He kneeled and blessed the God of Heaven. Then he hurried to the king and told him that he could show the dream and the interpretation of it. It was quite true, he said, that magicians and astrologers could not do it, but there was a God in Heaven who had revealed it to him. He said the king had seen a great image which had stood before him, with the head of fine gold, breast and arms of silver, belly and thighs of brass, legs of iron, and his feet of iron and of clay. Then the king had seen a stone that was cut out without hands which struck the image upon his feet and broke them to pieces. The rest of the image was destroyed like chaff and the wind carried all the pieces away. The stone became a great mountain and filled the earth.

Then Daniel told the interpretation, which was that the king was the head of gold, that other empires would follow, one of silver, one of iron, one of clay and iron, which would be weak and divided, until finally God would set up a Kingdom which would never be destroyed.

The king fell upon his knees and worshiped Daniel; he gave him many gifts and made him ruler over the whole province of Babylon.

The Feast of Belshazzar

BELSHAZZAR the king, the son of Nebuchadnezzar, made a great feast to a thousand of his lords and drank wine before the thousand. He ordered the golden and silver vessels which his father had brought from the temple at Jerusalem to be brought forth, and he and his guests drank wine out of them, meanwhile praising the gods of gold, of silver, of brass, of iron, of wood, and of stone.

As they were feasting, the fingers of a man's hand appeared and wrote upon the wall of the king's palace. The king saw the hand and the handwriting. He was frightened and troubled. He called the soothsayers, and quickly asked the meaning of the writing. He promised great rewards to anyone who could interpret the handwriting.

All the wise men came and looked at it, but it was in a language which they could not read; and the king was more troubled and excited than before. At length the queen came to the banquet house and said that in the days of his father, Nebuchadnezzar, there was a man in the kingdom who had great light and understanding and wisdom, and she suggested that Daniel be called to give the interpretation.

So Belshazzar called Daniel, and promised him robes of

purple, a chain of gold about his neck, and the position of third ruler in the kingdom if he could read the writing and make known the meaning of it.

Daniel said, "Let the gifts be for yourself, and give your rewards to another; yet I will read the handwriting and make known the interpretation."

Everyone listened while Daniel said:

"Thou hast, O king, lifted thyself up against the Lord of Heaven, and they have brought the vessels of His house before thee, and drunk wine from them. Thou hast praised the gods of silver, gold, brass, iron, wood, and stone, which see not, nor hear, nor know; and the God in whose hand thy breath is, and to Whom all thy ways belong thou hast not glorified."

The hand had disappeared, but the writing was there, and this is what it was: MENE, MENE, TEKEL, UPHARSIN.

This is Daniel's interpretation:

Mene: God hath numbered thy kingdom and finished it.

Tekel: Thou art weighed in the balances, and art found wanting.

Upharsin or Peres: Thy kingdom is divided, and is given to the Medes and Persians.

The king Belshazzar did as he had promised, and they clothed Daniel with scarlet, and put a chain of gold about his neck, and made a proclamation which said that he should be the third ruler in the kingdom.

That night Belshazzar, the king of the Chaldeans, was slain. Darius, the Median, took the kingdom and ruled it.

Daniel in the Lion's Den

DARIUS set an hundred and twenty princes over the whole kingdom, and over this number of princes, he established three presidents, of whom Daniel was the first. Darius showed such marked preference for Daniel because of his excellent spirit, that the other presidents and princes were jealous. They tried to find fault with Daniel, but they could not, for he was good and faithful, and there was no error or fault in him.

So they planned and plotted to see whether they could accomplish their destruction of Daniel by some other means.

They knew that Darius would hear no evil of Daniel, and they knew, too, that he was really a very vain person, easily flattered.

So they went to him and said: "We have all consulted together to establish a royal statute that whosoever shall ask a petition of any man or God for thirty days, save of thee, O king, he shall be cast into the den of lions." Then they asked the king to sign it, for according to the law of the Medes and Persians, once a thing is decreed, it cannot be changed. They knew that it was a daily habit of Daniel's to kneel at the windows of his house and give thanks to God three times a day, but they were very careful not to mention this to the king, for then he would not have signed the decree.

They watched carefully after the signing of the decree, and they saw Daniel kneeling by his window in prayer, as was his custom.

So they hurried to the king, and told him what they had seen. They reminded him that whoever prayed to anyone but Darius himself was to be thrown to the den of lions, and they demanded that this penalty be invoked against Daniel.

When the king heard their complaint, he was sadly displeased with himself, for he knew that he had been tricked. All day he thought of some way to keep Daniel from the lion's den; but there was no way, for the law of the Medes and Persians could not be changed. There was nothing left for Darius to do but to give the command that Daniel should be thrown to the lions.

Then the king spoke to Daniel and said, "Thy God, whom thou servest continually, he will deliver thee."

A stone was brought and laid upon the mouth of the den, and the king sealed it with his own signet and with that of his lords. Then he went sadly into his palace and passed the night fasting and wakeful.

Early the next morning he arose and went in haste to the lion's den. He cried out sorrowfully to Daniel, to ask him whether his God had been able to deliver him from the lions.

Daniel answered the king and said, "O king, live for ever.

My God hath sent his angel and hath shut the lions' mouths, and they have not hurt me."

Then was the king exceedingly glad for him and commanded that they should take Daniel up out of the lions' den. There was not a single mark upon Daniel, because he had believed in his God.

The king commanded that the men who had accused Daniel should themselves be thrown to the lions. Since they had no God to protect them, the lions tore them to bits before they reached the bottom of the den.

Esther became the queen of King Xerxes (*Story on page 112*).

Daniel was unharmed in the lion's den (*Story on page 128*).

God warned Joseph, in a dream, to flee into Egypt with Mary and the infant Jesus (*Story on page 139*).

Jesus in the temple talking with the learned doctors (*Story on page 143*).

Jonah Cast into the Sea

IN the days of Jeroboam the Second there was a prophet named Jonah. And God bade him go to Nineveh, and tell its inhabitants that He was going to destroy it for their great wickedness. But Jonah was not willing to go; and, thinking that he could escape God's notice, he hastened to Joppa, and took ship for Tarshish.

God was displeased with Jonah for all this, and caused so violent a storm to arise that the ship was in danger of being wrecked. Then the seamen drew lots to find out for whose wickedness this storm had come upon them, and the lot fell upon Jonah. So he told them all: and said that they must take him and throw him into the sea. The sailors were unwilling to do this. So they rowed hard, in hopes of getting to land. But it was of no use, so they had to throw Jonah over; and immediately the storm ceased.

But Jonah was not drowned. God had prepared a great fish, that swallowed him up, and at the end of three days swam to shore, and brought him up unhurt.

Then he went at once, and warned the Ninevites who repented of their sins, so that God spared their city.

Angels Appearing to the Shepherds

BEFORE God created Adam and Eve, He knew that they would disobey Him, and so ruin themselves. But the love that He had both for them, and for all human beings who should come after them, was so great, that He determined to save them from their miserable condition. The way in which God chose to do so was this—that His own Son should become a human being like ourselves; and, after having shown us how God's commands ought to be obeyed by His creatures, should die for us, that we might live forever with God in heaven.

The birth into the world of our Lord Jesus Christ took place in this way:

There was a woman named Mary living at Nazareth in Galilee. And the angel Gabriel appeared to her, saying, "Hail, thou that art highly favored, the Lord is with thee; blessed art thou among women."

Mary was afraid when she saw the angel. But he said, "Fear not, Mary; for thou hast found favor with God."

The angel told Mary that she should have a son, who should indeed be the son of God, the Savior of the world, who had so long been expected by His people.

After some time a decree was issued by Caesar Augustus that everyone should be enrolled. This meant that every man, with his wife and family, must go to the city of his birth to pay his taxes. Joseph, the husband of Mary, had to go up from Galilee, into Judea, to the city of David, which was called Bethlehem. Joseph, you see, was of the house and family of David.

The city was so crowded that there was no room for Mary and Joseph in the inn, but they found a place to sleep in a stable. It was in this little stable that our Lord was born. Mary wrapped him in swaddling clothes and laid him in a manger.

Now there were shepherds in the fields of Bethlehem, keeping watch over their flocks by night. And the angel of the Lord appeared to them in great glory, amid a bright light shining from heaven. And they were much afraid. But he bade them fear not, for he had brought them good tidings of a Savior, Christ the Lord, who was that day born in Bethlehem. And he told the shepherds that they should find the babe wrapped up in the manger, where his mother had laid him.

Then, suddenly, there was with him a multitude of other angels, praising God, and singing aloud, "Glory to God in the highest, and on earth peace, good-will toward men."

The shepherds wondered among themselves and said to one another, "Let us now go to Bethlehem, and see this thing which has happened, which the Lord has made known to us."

An angel appeared to Mary, saying, "Blessed art thou among women, for thou hast found favor with the Lord. He has chosen you to be the mother of His only begotten son."

When the angels had ascended up again into heaven, the shepherds hastened to Bethlehem, and there found Joseph and Mary, and the babe lying in a manger.

The shepherds fell on their knees to worship, and all who heard their story wondered at the things that had come to pass.

And they spread abroad the good news they had heard; and returned to their flocks, giving thanks to God.

The Naming of Jesus

WHEN eight days had passed, it was time for the little baby to be given His name. He was called Jesus, for an angel had appeared to Joseph in his sleep one night and told him that the baby should be called Jesus.

After some time had passed, Mary and Joseph and the baby Jesus left Bethlehem and went to Jerusalem, to present Him to the Lord. In those days it was the custom to take every boy child to the temple and tell God that He was to serve Him.

In the temple was an old man Simeon, who was very wise and good. The Holy Spirit had told him that he should not die until he had seen the Lord's Christ.

When Mary and Joseph walked into the temple, Simeon went up to them and took the babe in his arms. He said, "Blessed be the Lord, for He has let me see this wonderful child, who is to bring light to the whole world. Now I can depart in peace."

When Mary and Joseph had done everything according to the law of the Lord, they returned to Galilee, to their own city of Nazareth.

In the East three wise men saw the star which moved before them and led them on to Bethlehem, to the stable where the newborn baby lay.

The Offerings of the Wise Men

OTHER nations as well as the Jews had long been expecting the birth of a great and wonderful king, who should reign over all people upon the earth. The prophet Balaam, whom Balak sent for to curse the Israelites, and whom God caused to bless them instead, had spoken of Him as a Star rising out of Jacob; and owing to this, the appearance of a star had been looked for to show the time of His birth.

Now, when Jesus was born in Bethlehem, wise men, living in a distant country of the East, saw a remarkable star in the heavens, which seemed to point out the way to Jerusalem. So they came there, and inquired where He was who was born King of the Jews; for they had seen His star in the east, and were come to worship Him. The people of the city, together with Herod their king, were greatly troubled when they heard these words. So Herod called together the chief priests, and the most learned men in Jerusalem, and asked them where it was that the Christ was expected to be born. They told him in Bethlehem of Judea; for there was an old prophecy that out of that city should come one who was to rule over Israel.

Then Herod sent for the wise men; and after he had questioned them about this star which they had seen, he bade them go to Bethlehem, find out the young child, and bring him word, that he too might go and worship Him. So they went to Bethlehem, which was only a few miles off. And as they went, the star, which they had seen in their own far-off country in the east, moved on before them, till it stood over where the young child was. And when they came to Him, they kneeled down before Him, and gave Him rich gifts of gold and silver, and other precious things, in token of their duty and subjection to Him.

Now when Herod had desired the wise men to bring him word where the young child was, that he might go and worship Him, he had deceived them: he did not want to worship Him, but to kill Him; for, as Jesus was called King of the Jews, Herod feared that he might some day take his kingdom from him. God, who knows every thing, even the very thoughts that men imagine they are hiding in their hearts, knew how wickedly Herod was intending to act. So in a dream He told the wise men not to return to him. And they therefore went back again to their own country by another way.

Herod ordered the wise men to come before him, and he questioned them closely about the prophecy and the strange star.

The Flight into Egypt

HEROD waited anxiously for the return of the wise men. But when he found they had gone home again without coming to him, as he had told them, he was in a furious rage. And, in order to make sure that the child Jesus should not escape him, he sent out his soldiers to kill all the young children under two years old, not only in Bethlehem itself, but in all the country round about it. Oh, what weeping and lamenting were there, when the cruel king killed all their little ones!

But God had provided for the safety of Him who was indeed the Son of God, though He was thought to be the son of Joseph, Mary's husband. After the wise men had left Bethlehem, God sent an angel to Joseph, to bid him take the young child and His mother, and escape with them into the land of Egypt, because Herod sought Jesus on purpose to kill Him. The angel told him this in a dream. But Joseph knew that God had sent him; so they immediately fled for their lives into Egypt. There they lived for a number of years content to wait there since it was God's wish. Little is known of their days in Egypt. Nor did they return to their own

Herod waits in vain for the return of the wise men.

country till the angel, as he had said he would, again came to Joseph, in a dream, and told him that, as the wicked king was dead, they might now go back to their own home.

It was good news and having had the word of God they could scarce wait to return. Egypt had been a refuge but Judea was home.

Then they joyfully set out on their journey to the land of Israel. But when they got there, and found that one of Herod's sons, who was as wicked and cruel as his father, reigned over Judea in his place, Joseph was afraid of going thither. God, however, directed him, in a dream, to go to another part of the country of the Jews, called Galilee, which was many miles from Jerusalem, where Archelaus, the king that Joseph feared, was reigning. Galilee also was governed by a milder ruler than Judea was. His name was Antipas, and, though he was brother to Archelaus, there was no friendship between them. So there was every thing to make it safe for the Holy Family to go and live there.

When Joseph and Mary, with their child, came, by God's direction, into Galilee, they took up their abode in a city called Nazareth, which was henceforth the home of our blessed Lord.

And the child Jesus grew up in health and strength, with understanding far above that of a common child. And God His Father blessed Him exceedingly.

Jesus is taken to Nazareth.

Christs Disputing with the Doctors

OSEPH and Mary, the parents of our Lord, went to Jerusalem every year at the Feast of the Passover. This feast, or festival, was observed by the Jews in order to keep in mind their deliverance, by Moses, out of bondage in the land of Egypt, and to give thanks to God for it. God Himself had commanded them to keep this feast at Jerusalem; and, however toilsome or inconvenient the journey thither might be, still they went because He had bidden it. It lasted eight days; for it was a time not only to worship God with great solemnity, but for friends and families to rejoice together when they met from all parts of the country at Jerusalem.

When our Lord was twelve years old, His parents took Him with them when they went, as usual, to Jerusalem. But when all was over, and they were returning home in company with great numbers of other Jews, traveling together for safety in the wild parts of the country, they suddenly missed the child Jesus. They had not got far from Jerusalem when they missed Him; so, supposing Him to be with some of their friends, they went on several miles farther without feeling uneasy. But when they at last came to seek Him, He was nowhere to be found; and then, in great alarm, they hastened back to the city to look for Him. For three whole days they did not know what had become of Him. At length, when they did find Him, it was in the Temple, sitting among the doctors, or learned men of the Jews, who were all wondering at the way in which this child twelve years old talked with them concerning the law of God, which they were there to teach, and of which He knew so much more than they did. His mother told Him in what sorrow they had been about Him, and asked Him why He had thus distressed them by staying behind without their knowledge. But His answer amazed her still more; for He asked her why they had sought Him; did they not know that He must be about His Father's business? Mary did not know what He meant. But He spoke of God, who was His real Father, and who had sent Him into the world to teach, as well as to save it.

Nevertheless, when He had thus spoken, He followed her, and went back again with them to Nazareth, where He was obedient to them, like any other son; working at His father's trade, which was that of a carpenter.

John Baptizing Christ

ABOUT thirty years after the birth of our Lord, an extraordinary prophet, or teacher, appeared among the Jews. His name was John, and he was the son of Elizabeth, Mary's cousin. His father, Zacharias, was a priest.

One day, as Zacharias was ministering in the Temple, an angel of the Lord appeared to him. Zacharias was a very good man; still he was afraid when he saw this glorious being before him. But the angel bade him not fear, for he was come to tell him that God had heard his prayer, and would give him a son, who would not only make him happy, but be a cause of joy to many whom he should turn from their ill-doings to righteous ways. Zacharias was so amazed that he could scarcely believe what the angel said to him. But the angel told him that he was Gabriel, sent by God Himself to tell him this; and because Zacharias had not believed him, he should be dumb, and unable to speak till the birth of his child.

The people who were praying in another part of the Temple were surprised that Zacharias was so long in coming

DOME OF THE ROCK, TEMPLE AREA,
JERUSALEM

THE HEALING OF THE MULTITUDES

(Matt. 15: 29-31)

The beauty of soft, golden light from the setting sun illuminates a scene of infinite compassion. The Master lifts his hand in welcome to those who seek his help to free them from their suffering.

Lovingly He waits to receive "the lame, blind, dumb, maimed, and many others." Each one seeks Christ with hope. Their expectancy is reflected by the expressions on their faces. On this hillside far above the sea of Galilee where the sick in spirit have been healed, He now heals those who are ill of body.

The blind, the crippled, the suffering — every one made "whole" again, by the healing presence of Christ.

A SYNAGOGUE AT CAPERNAUM
AS IT IS TODAY.

to them. When he did come, they perceived that something strange had happened to him, for he could only make signs to them instead of speaking. Afterward he returned to his own home, where he remained dumb till the birth of the son that had been promised to him. Then, when they came to name the child, and Zacharias had written that he must be called John (for so the angel had said), suddenly his dumbness left him, and he gave thanks aloud to God.

When John grew up, God sent him to tell the Jews that they must repent, and amend their lives. Great numbers thronged to the wilderness of Judea, where he dwelt, clad in coarse garments, and living on locusts and wild honey. And when he bade them repent, for the kingdom of heaven was at hand, they confessed their sins, and were baptized by him in the River Jordan.

The crowds kept asking John, "What must we do?"

He answered, "Let him who has two coats share with him who has none; and let him who has food give to him that has none."

The tax-payers came to be baptized, and they said, "Teacher, what must we do?"

John answered, "Do not take more from any one than rightfully belongs to you."

Soldiers came to be baptized, and they said, "And what must we do?"

And he answered, "Do not take money from anybody by force, nor make false charges, but be content with what is justly coming to you."

People began to wonder whether John might possibly be the Christ, but he denied it, and told them of the coming of a Mightier One, whose shoe-strings he was not worthy to untie.

Jesus Himself came to John to be baptized; but John, knowing that He was indeed the Son of God, earnestly forbade Him. Jesus, however, told him that it was the will of God that it should be so; and then John baptized Him in the River Jordan.

When Jesus came up from the river and was praying, John saw the heavens opened, and the Spirit of God, in shape like a dove, descending, and resting upon Jesus. And there was heard a voice from heaven, of God Himself, saying, "This is my beloved Son, in whom I am well pleased."

Jesus Goes into the Wilderness

ESUS went alone into the wilderness, after He was baptized by John, and fasted there for forty days and forty nights, and was hungry.

Then the devil came to Him and said, "If you are the Son of God, command these stones to become bread."

But Jesus answered, "It is written that man is not to live on bread alone, but on the word of God as well."

Then the devil transported him to the holy city and set Him down on the highest point of the Temple. He said, "If you are the Son of God, throw yourself down; for it is written that He will give His angels charge of you."

Jesus answered, "Yes, but it is also written that you shall not tempt the Lord your God."

Then the devil took Him to a high mountain and showed Him all the kingdoms of the world and their power and wealth. He said, "I will give you all of these things if you will fall down and worship me."

Jesus answered, "Away with you, Satan! for it is written that you shall worship only God and serve Him alone."

The First Four Apostles

EROD seized John the Baptist and threw him into prison because John tried to dissuade him from wrong-doing.

After John was put in prison, Jesus came into Galilee, preaching God's good news.

As He was passing along the shore of the Sea of Galilee, on His way to Capernaum, where He went to live, He saw Simon and Andrew, his brother, casting their nets into the sea. They were fishermen, and Jesus said to them, "Come with me, and I will make you fishers of men."

At once they left their nets and followed Him.

As they went on a little farther, they saw James and John, sons of Zebedee, who were in their boat mending their nets. He spoke to them too, and at once they left their nets, and followed Him.

Water Turned into Wine

WHEN John baptized the multitudes who came to him in the wilderness of Judea, he told them there was One coming after him, mightier than he, and who should give them a better baptism than his. He spoke of Jesus, the Christ; for God had sent John not only to bid the Jews repent, but to tell them that He, who had so long been spoken of by their prophets as the Messiah, was about to appear among them.

Some thought John himself was this Messiah. But he denied it earnestly when they asked him; and pointing out to them Jesus, told them He was the Son of God who was to take away the sins of the world.

Then from one to another it began to be talked of that the Messiah was actually come. Some of those who heard this went to Jesus Himself, to make quite sure that it was true. And when they had seen Him, and heard Him explain what their prophets had said concerning Him, they believed that He was indeed their Messiah.

After His baptism by John, Jesus returned to His own country, Galilee. And He began to teach the people, and to do many wonderful works, called miracles, in order to show them that He was the Son of God.

The first miracle that Jesus did was at Cana, a town in Galilee, at a wedding, to which He, His mother, and some of His friends were invited. There was a large number of guests at this wedding, and when they were at supper (for an Eastern wedding takes place at night) they found they had not wine enough. Mary told this to Jesus; and, judging from His answer that He would in some wonderful way supply their want, she bade the servants do whatever He might command them. Presently Jesus told the servants to fill with water the large stone water-pots that were standing by. So they filled them quite full. Then He bade them draw it out, and carry it to the governor of the feast—that is, the one who had the care of providing for the guests. And when he tasted (not knowing what Jesus had done), he found it such excellent wine, that he called to the bridegroom, telling him that people generally brought out their best wine first, and afterward that which was worse; but he had kept his best wine till the last.

Then those who saw this miracle that Christ had done, of turning water into wine, felt still more convinced than they had been before that this was indeed the Messiah.

Christel Heals the Ten Lepers

AS Jesus and His disciples were on their way to Jerusalem, they passed through Samaria and Galilee. In a certain village they were met by ten lepers, who approached until they were within sound of voice. Then they cried out in despair, "Jesus, Master, have pity on us."

Jesus said to them, "Go, and show yourselves to the priests."

So they went as He had commanded them, and they were made clean and whole again.

One of them, when he saw that he was healed, turned back and sought Jesus again. He fell down at the feet of Jesus with his face to the ground, and thanked him, praising God in a loud voice.

Jesus saw that this man was not one of his own countrymen, but was a Samaritan; and He said, "Were not ten made clean? Where are the other nine? Was there no one returned to give thanks to God except this stranger?"

And to the man Jesus said, "Arise and go on your way. Your faith has made you well."

Christ Driving Out the Money-Changers

AFTER the miracle at Cana, Jesus, with His mother, His relations, and many of those who believed Him to be the Messiah, or Christ, went up to Jerusalem to keep the Feast of the Passover.

The Temple in Jerusalem was a most magnificent building, erected by King Herod; for the Temple that Solomon built had long been destroyed, as well as the one raised by Ezra, after the return of the Jews from their captivity in Babylon. It was built in courts, one within another, each inner court rising above the next outer one, like a terrace; so that the Temple itself, which was the innermost, was the highest of all, and could be seen from all parts of the city. The whole of these buildings belonging to the Temple covered a great space; for the outer court was nearly half a mile round.

When Christ went to the Temple, He found sad misdoings in this outer court; for it had been turned into a sort of market-place. Dealers in oxen, and sheep, and doves were selling their beasts and birds there; and money-changers, that is, those whose business was to supply strangers in Jerusalem with coin that was used there in exchange for their foreign money, carried on their trade within it. This was a profane thing; that is, it was not treating the place where God had appointed that He should be worshiped with the reverence with which it ought to be treated. And Jesus, when He saw it, was so angry, that, making a scourge, or whip of small cords, He drove all these people away, together with their oxen, and sheep, and doves, bidding them not make His Father's house a house of merchandise. And He overthrew the tables at which the money-changers were sitting, scattering their money all abroad.

The Jews, who looked on, were astonished to see Jesus turning these merchants out of the place where they had been accustomed to carry on their business; for He did it like one who had a right to drive them away. And they asked Him what miracle He could do, in order to show that God had sent Him.

He answered, "Destroy this Temple, and in three days I will raise it up."

The Jews, not understanding this, treated Him with contempt, saying that the Temple had been forty-six years in building; did He think He could rear it up again in three days? But He spoke of His own body; for He was to be put to death for the sins of the world, and brought to life again in three days after.

Healing the Man at the Pool

JESUS went to a festival of the Jews in Jerusalem. There was a pool beside the sheep gate. It was called Bethesda. On its five porches were lying or sitting people who were sick or blind or lame, for it was believed that at certain times when the water in the pool was troubled, an angel of the Lord came and ruffled the pool. The first person who stepped into the water after it was stirred was made well, no matter what illness he had.

One man who was ill had been there for thirty-eight years. Jesus saw him lying there, and he could see that the man had been ill for a long time.

He went to the man and said, "Do you want to be made well?"

The sick man said, "Yes, sir, but I have no one to look after me or to put me into the pool when the water is stirred. You see, I am hardly able to move, and someone else always gets in before I can."

Jesus said, "Arise, take up your bed, and walk."

Immediately the man was well and took up his bed and walked.

Christ and the Woman of Samaria

ROM Jerusalem, Jesus went into the country round about, teaching and baptizing the people. Afterward He returned to Galilee again.

To go thither, Jesus had to pass through Samaria, which was another part of Palestine. As He traveled on in Samaria He came to a city called Sychar, near to the piece of ground that Jacob gave to his son Joseph, and where there was a well that Jacob himself had digged. In that hot country, the digging a well was so great a service to all the people round about it that it was often called by the name of him who had dug it, and so this one was called Jacob's well. It was about the middle of the day, and Jesus, being wearied with His journey, sat down by the well to rest, while His disciples went into the city to buy food. As He sat there, a woman came to draw water, and He asked her to let Him drink. The woman, perceiving that He was a Jew, was surprised at His asking her for water; for the Jews so hated the Samaritans that they would neither eat, drink, nor sit down with them. And she asked Jesus how it was that He asked her, a Samaritan, for water. Jesus answered her, that if she knew who it was that had begged her to give Him water, she would rather have asked it of Him, and He would have given her living water. By "living water" He meant those great blessings which He had come into the world to bestow upon all people in it. But the woman, not knowing what He meant, told Him that the well was very deep, and He had no bucket to draw with, so that He could not give her drink of the fresh, springing water. Jesus answered her that those who drank of that well would be thirsty again, but those who drank of the living water that He should give them should thirst no more. The woman still did not understand Him; but thinking it was some very excellent water, begged that He would give it to her, that she might not have the trouble of coming, day by day, to the well to draw.

Then Jesus talked with her, to teach her what He meant; and He told her that He was the Messiah, whom the Samaritans were expecting as well as the Jews. And the woman believed Him; and leaving her water-pot, went to the city to bid the people there come and see Him who was surely the Christ. And many in that place, when they had seen and heard Jesus, believed on Him as the Savior of the world.

Christer Restores the Widow's Son

JESUS was passing through the town, followed by His disciples and a great crowd of people. As they reached the gate of the town, He saw one who was dead being carried out. He was the only son of his mother, who was a widow. Many of the people of the town were mourning with her.

When Jesus saw her, He was moved and said to her, "Do not weep."

And He came and touched the coffin, saying, "Young man, I say to you, arise."

Then the man who had been dead sat up and began to speak, and Jesus said to the mother, "Here is your son again."

The people were filled with wonder and cried out in praise to God, saying, "A great prophet has come among us, and God has visited his people."

And the story of what Jesus had done was told all through Judea.

He Cures a Man Who Cannot Walk

WHEN Jesus returned to Capernaum again, so many people came to see Him that there was no more room for them in the room, not even at the door. While Jesus was speaking to them, four men came, carrying a fifth man who was paralyzed and who could not move. They could not get near to Jesus because of the throng around Him; so they removed some of the material from the roof above His head. When they had made a hole large enough, they let down the bed upon which the sick man was lying.

Jesus knew that what they had done was because of their faith in Him, and He said, "Son, your sins are forgiven."

But some of the scribes who were sitting there watching said among themselves, "Why should this man say such a thing? He is being blasphemous! No one can forgive sins except God alone."

Jesus knew what they were saying and said to them, "Why do you say that? Which is easier—to say to this man, 'Your sins are forgiven'; or to say 'Get up, take your bed and walk'?

But so that you will know that the Son of Man has the power to forgive sins on earth, I will say to you, 'Rise, take up your bed and go home.' "

Then the man stood up and picked up his bed and went out, and all of the people were filled with wonder and praised God, saying, "We have never seen anything like this."

The Sermon on the Mount

THEN Jesus went again to Cana in Galilee, where He had changed water into wine.

Now there was a certain nobleman at Capernaum, whose son had been ill, and was now dying. And when his father heard that Jesus was at Cana, he went thither to beg Him to come and cure his son. Jesus at first seemed unwilling to grant his request; but the nobleman only the more earnestly entreated Him to come with him at once, lest his son should be dead before they reached Capernaum. Then Jesus bade him return home, for his son was already restored to health. The nobleman, believing that it was as Jesus said, immediately set out to go to Capernaum; and on the way he met his servants coming to tell him that his son was well. He asked them at what time he had begun to amend. They answered that the fever had left him at a certain hour the day before. So his father knew that was just the time when Jesus had told him that his son was well. And he and all his household, seeing this great miracle, believed on Jesus as the Savior whom God had sent into the world.

When Jesus returned to his own city, Nazareth, He went

Jesus came to John to be baptized (*Story on page 146*).

Jesus saw James and John, the sons of Zebedee, in their boat mending their nets, and he called to them to leave their fishing and come with him, for he said, "I will make you fishers of men" (*Story on page 148*).

Jesus asked the woman of Samaria for water (*Story on page 155*).

As Jesus walked along the road, he knew that someone in the crowd touched him to be healed, for he could feel some of the power go out of him. A sick woman had kissed the hem of his garment (*Story on page 166*).

on the Sabbath-day into the synagogue (a place where the Jews worshipped God), and, as His custom was, stood up to read the Scriptures to the people. He read to them in the book of Isaiah; and, when He had done reading, and closed the book, He spoke to them of Himself as the Messiah, of whom the prophet Isaiah wrote. The people heard Him gladly at first; but when He went on to speak to them of their misdoings, they rose up against Him in a rage, drove Him violently out of the city, and would have killed Him by throwing Him down from a steep part of the hill on which Nazareth stood. But He, by His wonderful power, quietly withdrew Himself from their fury, and came to Capernaum, where He afterward lived.

Then Jesus went about through Galilee, teaching the people, and working great miracles. And vast numbers from every part of Palestine came to hear Him, and to be cured of all kinds of diseases.

Then, seeing the multitude thronging around Him, He sat down on the hill-side near Capernaum, and taught them holy teaching, such as they had never before heard. And they were filled with astonishment; for He taught them like one whom God had indeed sent to them, and who must be obeyed.

New Wine into New Skins

ONCE the disciples of John and the Pharisees were keeping a fast, but the disciples of Jesus were not keeping a fast. People came to Jesus and began to ask Him why His disciples did not observe a fast also.

Jesus answered, "Can guests at a wedding fast while the bridegroom is with them? As long as they have the bridegroom, they cannot fast. But the time will come when he is taken away from them, and then they will fast. No one sews a piece of new cloth on an old coat, lest the patch break away from it, the new from the old, and the tear be made worse. No one pours new wine into old wine-skins lest the new wine burst the skins and both the wine and the wine-skins be lost. Instead, new wine is poured into fresh wine-skins."

Another time when Jesus was questioned was on a Sabbath when He and His disciples were walking through the grain-fields. The disciples began to pull off the heads of the grain.

The Pharisees asked, "Sir, why are your disciples doing things on the Sabbath which are unlawful?"

And Jesus answered, "The Sabbath was made for man,

and not man for the Sabbath; so that the Son of Man is master even of the Sabbath."

And yet another time the Pharisees questioned what Jesus did on the Sabbath. He went into a synagogue, where there was a man whose hand was shrivelled. The man stretched forth his hand for help, and Jesus said, "Rise and come forward."

The people watched closely to see whether He could heal the man on the Sabbath day.

Jesus knew what they were thinking, and He said, "Is it lawful to do good or harm on the Sabbath day? If you have but one sheep and it fall into a hole on the Sabbath day, would you not take hold of it and lift it out? Is not a man of much greater value than a sheep?"

There was no answer, and Jesus looked sorrowful because they had so little pity and sympathy for the man.

Then He said, "Stretch out your hand," and the hand was made whole and well.

Christt Stilling the Tempest

WHEN our Lord came down from the rising ground, from which He had been speaking to the people, great numbers followed Him. Among them was a man afflicted with a most dreadful disease, that no one in that country had ever been able to cure, and of which the Jews were so much afraid that they would not touch the person suffering from it. This man came and worshiped Jesus, entreating Him to cure him. And Jesus laid His hand upon him; and the disease left him in that very moment.

Jesus bade the man not tell any one how he had been cured; but the man went about telling every one, so that Jesus dared not show Himself in the city for fear of the chief people. So He remained in the open country, where people from every part came to Him to be cured of their diseases.

Capernaum, which was now the home of our Lord, was a town standing on the borders of the Lake of Gennesareth. This lake was a very large one; indeed, quite a sea, abounding with fish, and having many towns and villages on its coast. Our Lord was one day teaching the people by the side of this lake, and they pressed so close upon Him that He got into one of the fishing-boats that lay on the shore, and told Simon, to whom it belonged, to push out a little from the land. And then He spoke to the people from the boat, as they crowded to the water's edge.

After He had done speaking, He told Simon to launch out into deep water, and let down his net to catch fish. Simon thought it was of no use to do so, for they had been hard at work all night, and had caught nothing; yet, as Jesus bade him, he would let down the net once more. So they cast their net into the sea, and, to their astonishment, caught so much fish that they were obliged to call fishermen from another boat to help them. And when they had got their boat to land, they left everything, that they might be always with Christ.

Then Jesus took boat with His disciples to go to the other side of the lake. But after they had put out to sea a storm arose, so violent that the vessel was filled with the waves dashing over it. And, in great terror, thinking they should be lost, the disciples came and awoke Jesus, who was asleep. And they cried out, "Master, Master, save us!" Then He arose, and by a word stilled the winds and the waves, so that there was a great calm. And He asked His disciples how they could think that He would leave them to perish!

Christt Raising Jairus' Daughter

WHEN Jesus was at Capernaum again, one day, when He was teaching the people, there came to Him the ruler, or chief man, of one of the Jewish synagogues. And he entreated Jesus to come and save his little daughter, who was dying. Jesus went with him immediately, followed by many of the people, who crowded around Him.

In the crowd was a woman who had been ill for twelve years and none of her physicians could heal her. She came behind Jesus and touched the border of His garment. Immediately she was well again.

Jesus said, "Who touched me?"

Everyone denied having done so, until Peter, who was with Him said, "Master, people are thronging about you and pressing from all sides. So why do you ask who touched you?"

Jesus explained that someone had touched Him in a different way, for He felt some of the virtue go out of Him.

Then the woman saw that she could not hide; so she came trembling, and falling down before Him, she told how and for what reason she had touched Him, and how she had been healed at once.

Jesus said, "Daughter, be of good comfort. Thy faith hath made thee whole. Go in peace."

As He spoke, the servants of the ruler came to meet him, and tell him that his daughter was dead, so that it was in vain for Jesus to come to her. When Jesus heard this, He comforted Jairus (that was the name of the ruler), bidding him not fear, but trust to Him. Then, taking with Him Peter, James, and John, His disciples, they went into the ruler's house, where all was grief and confusion; friends and neighbors weeping and lamenting over the poor dead child. Jesus asked them why they wept and lamented so sadly; for the child was not dead, she was only sleeping. But as they did not understand what Jesus meant, and as they saw the poor child was dead, they only laughed at Him.

Then Jesus sent all these people away; and having with Him only the little girl's father and mother, and the three disciples, He went with them into the room where the child lay dead. Then He took her by the hand, and bade her arise. And immediately her spirit, which had left her body, came to it again, and she arose and walked about, well and strong; and He told them to give her something to eat. But, though He strictly commanded them not to tell any one what He had done, this wonderful work was heard of far and wide.

Jesus did not only teach, and work miracles Himself throughout the country of the Jews, but He gave power to do so to twelve of His disciples. These are called apostles;

and they were chosen to be always with Christ, that they might, after His death, be able to assure all men that He was indeed the Son of God.

Their names were, Simon, who is also called Peter; Andrew, his brother; and James and John, the sons of an old man named Zebedee. These four had been fishermen; and, while they were busy with their boats and nets, had been called by Christ to follow Him. Then there were Philip and Bartholomew; Thomas; Matthew; James, the uncle of our Lord; Lebbaeus, whose surname was Thaddaeus; another Simon, brother to James; and Judas Iscariot.

Jesus Visits Nazareth

JESUS went to visit Nazareth, where He had spent His boyhood. As was His custom He went on the Sabbath into the Synagogue and stood up to read the lesson. But as He was teaching, many who heard Him were astonished and said, "How can this be? Where did He get these teachings? How has this wisdom been given Him? and what are these miracles of healing that He does? For is He not the carpenter, the son of Mary and the brother of James and Joses and Judas and Simon? His sisters are living here among us."

And they would not believe in Him.

Jesus said, "A prophet is not without honor except in his own country and among his relatives and in his own home."

In Nazareth the people were so lacking in faith that He could do no wonderful acts except laying His hands on a few sick people and healing them. So He had to go into the villages near by to continue His teaching.

Christic Walking on the Sea

JOHN, who was called the Baptist, had now been put to death, because he told King Herod of his misdoings. But when the king heard of the wonderful works done by Christ, he was alarmed, and said that this must be John risen from the dead. So Jesus then left Capernaum, lest Herod should try to kill Him also, and went into the desert parts of Bethsaida, where multitudes followed to hear Him, and to be cured of their diseases.

Then, in the evening, the disciples came to Jesus, begging Him to send the people away, that they might go into the neighboring villages and buy food; for they had nothing to eat, and that was a desert place. Jesus answered the disciples that the people need not go away: they must give them food.

And they said, "Shall we go and buy two hundred pennyworth of bread, and give them something to eat?"

He said, "How many loaves have you? Go and see."

When they knew, they came back and said that they had five loaves of barley bread and two small fishes, and how could they divide that among so many people?

Then Jesus commanded them to make all of the people sit down by companies upon the green grass, by hundreds and by fifties. And when they had done so, He took the five loaves and the two fishes, and, looking up to heaven, gave thanks to God. Then, breaking the loaves and the fishes, He gave them to the disciples to set before the multitude. And they all ate, and had enough; and twelve baskets were filled with what was left. There were about five thousand men, besides women and children, whom Jesus fed in this way.

When they had done eating, Jesus desired His disciples to sail over to the other side of the lake, while He sent the people away.

But in the night a storm arose; and the disciples, who were at sea, were sadly tossed about, and almost spent with rowing against wind and waves. Then, as morning broke, they saw Jesus coming toward them, walking upon the sea. But they did not know that it was He; seeing Him move along upon the water, they thought it must be a spirit, and they cried out for fear.

Jesus, however, immediately spoke, and comforted them, saying, "It is I, be not afraid."

Then Peter answered, "Lord, if it be Thou, bid me come unto Thee upon the water."

Jesus bade him come: so Peter also walked upon the water. But when he saw how stormy it was, he was afraid, and, beginning to sink, cried out to Jesus to save him. And Jesus caught him, and held him up, asking him why he had doubted His power.

Then, as soon as they were both in the ship, the storm ceased.

Then those who were in the ship came and worshiped Him, saying, "Of a truth, Thou art the Son of God."

When they crossed over the water, they came to the land of Gennesarat. The people of that place heard of Him and sent out into the country all around for those who were ill and bed-ridden, who might come before Christ and be made whole.

Wherever He went, into the villages, or into the cities, or into the country, they laid the sick in the streets, and begged that they might touch Him, if it were only the hem of His garment. And all who touched Him were made perfectly whole.

The Good Samaritan

JESUS often taught the people by means of what are called parables. A parable is a kind of story, or fable; and the Jewish people, as well as those of other Eastern countries, were very fond of them.

One day, when Jesus was with His disciples, a lawyer, that is, a teacher of the law which Moses gave to the Jews, asked Him what he must do in order that he might live forever with God in heaven. He asked this, not because he wanted to know, but just to see what kind of answer Christ would give him. Jesus, in reply, asked him what was written in the law which God had given to them. The lawyer answered that the law told him that he must love God with all his heart, and mind, and soul, and strength; and that he must love his neighbor as well as he loved himself. Jesus told him that he had answered rightly; if he did so, he should live forever with God in heaven. But then the lawyer wanted to know who was his neighbor. And this Jesus taught him by means of a parable.

He said, A certain man, as he went from Jerusalem to Jericho, was set upon by thieves, who stripped him even of

173

his clothing, wounded him, and then went on, leaving him half dead.

And, as he lay there, a priest came along the same road; but, instead of stopping to help the wounded man as he ought to have done, he passed on, on the other side of the way. Next came a Levite, that is, an inferior kind of priest, who just looked at the poor man, and then went away, without doing any thing for him. Last of all, there was a Samaritan traveling on that road; but he, instead of passing on as the others had done, hastened to him, dressed and bound up his wounds, and then, setting him on the beast that he was himself riding, took him to an inn, where he got him food and lodging. Then the next day, when he went on his journey again, he gave some money to the landlord of the inn, bidding him take care of the wounded Jew, and telling him that if he spent any thing more he would repay him when he came back.

When Jesus had told the lawyer this story, He asked him which of the three was really neighbor to him who had been set upon by thieves; his own countrymen, or the Samaritan? The lawyer answered, he was his neighbor who had showed him such kindness.

Then Jesus told him to consider every man his neighbor who needed a kindness from him.

The Parable of the Sower

ONCE when Jesus was teaching beside the lake, such a large crowd came and gathered round Him that He entered a boat and was rowed out on the lake to speak to the people as they stood on the shore.

He said, "Once a sower went out to sow, and as he sowed, some of the seed fell on the road, where the birds came and ate it up.

"Some fell on rocky ground, where it had but little soil. Because there was no depth of good earth, it began to grow at once, but when the sun came out, it had no root to sustain it and soon it withered away.

"Some of the seed fell among the thorns, and the thorns grew up and choked it so that it soon died.

"Other seed fell on good soil, and sprouted and grew, and bore at the rate of thirty, sixty, and a hundredfold."

When the people had gone away, the disciples asked what the story meant.

He said, "Do you not see the meaning of it? Then how will you be able to understand my other stories? The sower is sowing his teaching. The teaching that is sown along the road is like some people who hear but Satan comes and takes it away immediately.

"The seed that has been sown on rocky places is like the people who hear the teaching with rejoicing, but it takes no root, and they forget immediately.

"The seed sown among thorns is like those who hear the teaching, but the pleasures of this life, the desire for wealth and other things makes them forget the teaching, and so it bears no fruit.

"But the seed sown on good soil is like those people who hear the teaching and remember it, and it bears fruit; some thirty, some sixty, and some a hundredfold."

DAMASCUS GATE IN NORTHERN WALL
OF JERUSALEM

THE FEEDING OF THE MULTITUDES
(John 6: 5-13)

It is late afternoon and the time is approaching to partake of food. Many people who came to see and hear Jesus neglected to bring food with them, and others had no food to bring. In response to the law of love as exemplified in Christ, a young boy willingly offers to share his five loaves and two fishes. Jesus accepts and blesses the food, and everyone follows the Christly example.

The atmosphere reflects a spirit of brotherly love and unselfish generosity. The fellowship with Christ and one another is enriched as they share their blessings. Before the sun will set, all will be abundantly fed, and there will be full baskets left over.

RUINS OF ANCIENT BABYLON, CENTRAL MESOPOTAMIA.

The Parable of the Talents

JESUS said, "The Kingdom of Heaven is like a man who before going abroad called his servants and gave what he had into their charge. To one he gave five talents, to another two, and to another one, each according to what he was able to do. Then he went on his journey.

"The servant who received five talents went immediately and traded with them and gained five more talents.

"The servant who had received two talents went out also and traded and made two more talents.

"But he who had received but one talent went out and dug a hole in the ground and in it he hid his master's money.

"When the master came back, the servants went to him to settle their accounts with him.

"The one who had received five talents said, 'Look, master, you gave me five talents and with them I earned five more.'

"His master said, 'Well done, good and faithful servant. You have been faithful over a few things, I will put you in charge of many things. Share your master's happiness.'

"The one who had received two talents came and said, 'Master, you gave me two talents, and with them I earned two more talents.'

"His master said, 'Well done, good and faithful servant. You have been faithful over a few things, I will put you in charge of many things. Share your master's happiness.'

"Then came the servant who had received but one talent, and he said, 'Master, I knew that you are a hard man, reaping where you have not sown, and gathering where you have not winnowed. So I was afraid and hid your talent in the ground. There you have what belongs to you.'

"But his master was displeased. 'Idle, worthless servant,' he said. 'You knew that I reap where I have not sown and gather where I have not winnowed. You ought, therefore, to have put my money in the hands of bankers and I would have received it with interest. Take my talent away from him and give it to the servant who has ten talents. For to every one who has shall be given and he shall have plenty; but from him who has only a little, even what he has shall be taken away. Throw this worthless old servant out.'"

Jesus and Zaccheus

ONCE as Jesus went through Jericho, a rich tax-gatherer named Zaccheus tried to see what Jesus looked like. The crowd was so great, however, that he could not get near Him, and he was very short so that he could not see over their heads. So Zaccheus ran on ahead and climbed into a sycamore tree on the road which Jesus must take.

When Jesus came to the place, He looked up and said to him, "Zaccheus, come down, for today I must stay at your house."

And Zaccheus came down quickly and welcomed Him most joyfully.

Many people in the crowd began to find fault with Jesus because He was going to eat with a man who was a sinner.

Zaccheus said, "Lord, I will give half of all that I have to the poor; and to every man whom I have cheated out of anything, I will give back four times as much."

Then Jesus said, "Today salvation has come to this house, for you have proved yourself to be a true son of Abraham. For the Son of Man came to seek and to save the lost."

The Blind Leading the Blind

NOTHER time Jesus said to His apostles, "Can a blind man lead a blind man? Will not both fall into a ditch? A disciple is not above his teacher; but every pupil perfectly trained will be like his teacher.

"No good tree bears rotten fruit. Nor does a rotten tree bear good fruit, for each tree is known by its own fruit. Figs are not gathered from thorns, nor grapes picked from a bramble-bush. A man brings forth good from the good stored in his heart, and an evil man brings forth evil from the evil stowed in his heart.

"You are the light of the world. A city on a hill cannot be hidden. One does not light a candle to put it under a basket but on a stand where it may give light to all who are in the house. So let your light shine before men that they may see your good deeds and praise your heavenly Father."

The Man Who Built on Rock

JESUS spoke to His disciples, saying, "Do not think that I came to set aside the old law or teachings of the prophets. I came not to set them aside, but to complete them.

"Come to me, all you who labor and are heavily burdened, and I will give you rest. Take my yoke upon you and learn of me, for I am kind and sympathetic, and you will find rest, for my yoke is easy and my burden is light.

"He who hears these words of mine and keeps them in mind will be like a wise man who built his house upon rock. The rain fell, the floods came, the winds blew and beat upon the house. But it did not fall, for its foundation was built on the rock.

"He who hears these words of mine but does not keep them in mind will be like the foolish man who built his house on sand. The rain fell, the floods came, the winds blew and beat upon the house, and it fell, and great was its downfall."

The Prodigal Son

AMONG those who came to hear Christ were heathens from various countries. A heathen is one who does not worship the true God. And these heathens Christ received as kindly as He did His own countrymen.

The chief men of the Jews were offended at this, for they thought themselves better than any other people in the world. So, to reprove them for their unkindness to these, who were God's children as well as they, Christ told them a parable.

He said, There was a man who had two sons; and the younger son demanded his share of his father's property. So his father divided all that he had between the two. The younger son then immediately took his share to a distant country, where he soon ruined himself by wasteful and riotous living. And when he had spent everything there arose a great famine in that land, and he was in such want that he hired himself to a countryman, who sent him into the fields to tend swine. Here he was so hungry that he would gladly have eaten what the swine were feeding upon, but no one gave him anything to eat. Then, when he saw to what a miserable condition he had brought himself, he envied even the servants in his father's house, for they had enough and to spare. And he determined that he would go home again to his father, confess how ill he had behaved, and, though he could not expect to be forgiven, entreat him to let him stay with him as a servant.

So he set out on his journey home; but when he was a great way off, his father saw him, ran lovingly to meet him, and kissed him again and again. Then he told his father that he had sinned against God, and against him, and was not fit to be called his son any more.

The father called to his servants and said, "Bring forth quickly the best robe and put it on him; and put a ring on his hand and shoes on his feet. And bring the fatted calf, and kill it, and let us eat and make merry."

And they began to be merry and to eat and rejoice together.

The elder son was in the field, where he had been working. As he came near the house, he heard music and dancing.

He called to one of the servants, and asked him how these things came to be.

The servant answered, "Thy brother is come. Thy father hath killed the fatted calf, because he is home again safe and sound."

Then the elder son was angry and would not go into the house. So his father came out to find out what the trouble was.

The elder son said, "Lo, these many years I have served thee, and never disobeyed. Yet thou never gavest me a kid, that I might make merry with my friends. But when this thy son came, who has wasted everything that was given to him, thou killest for him the fatted calf."

But his father answered him, "Son, thou art ever with me, and all that I have is thine. It was right that we should make merry and be glad; for this thy brother was dead, and is alive again; and was lost, and is found."

Christt Blessing Little Children

ONE day, after Christ had been teaching the people, little children were brought to Him that He might lay His hands on them and pray for them. His disciples, for some reason or other, found fault with those who brought them, and would have hindered them. But when Jesus knew what His disciples had done, He was much displeased with them for it. And He said to them, "Suffer little children to come unto me, and forbid them not; for of such is the kingdom of heaven." Then He took the little children lovingly in His arms, laid His hands upon them, and blessed them.

Our Lord had now been teaching and working miracles among the Jewish people for nearly three years and a half. Thousands upon thousands had seen the wonderful things that He did, and heard what He had to tell them concerning God their Father; and also concerning Himself, who was the Son of God, come into the world to save them. They did not understand all that He said, but many believed Him to be the long-promised Messiah.

But there were many wicked men among the Jews who

hated Christ; and their rulers and chief priests tried from time to time to lay hold of Him, that they might kill Him. God at last allowed them to have their own will in this; and Jesus was now on His last journey to Jerusalem, where He was to be put to death. He knew all that was to happen to Him there—all the shame and suffering that were to be inflicted upon Him. But He knew that it was the will of His Father that He should bear it; and He knew that it should be for the deliverance of all human creatures from the sad consequences of their sins against God. So He did not seek to avoid it.

The Lilies of the Field

JESUS said, "Do not be anxious about your life, nor about what you shall eat, or what you shall wear. For does not life mean more than food and the body more than clothing? Consider how the birds of the air neither sow nor reap nor gather into barns, and yet your heavenly Father feeds them. Are you not worth far more than they? Are not two sparrows sold for a penny? Yet not one of them falls to the ground without your Father's knowledge. As for you, the very hairs of your head are numbered. Then have no fear, for you are worth far more than the sparrows.

"Which of you by anxiety can add a single foot to his height? And why be anxious about what you wear? Consider the lilies of the field, how they grow. They toil not, neither do they spin, and yet not even Solomon in all his splendor was clothed like one of these. Now if God so clothes the grass of the field which is alive today but tomorrow is thrown into the oven, is it not far more certain that he will clothe you, O men of little faith?

"Do not be anxious then and say, 'What shall we eat or

what shall we drink or with what shall we be clothed?'
For all these things the heathen is seeking, but your
heavenly Father knows that you need all these things. Seek
first to do right as he would have you do, and all these other
things will be given to you. Therefore, do not be anxious
about tomorrow. Tomorrow will take care of itself."

The Rich Man and Heaven

NCE when Jesus was walking along a road, a man knelt suddenly before him and asked, "Good Master, what must I do to be sure of eternal life?"

Jesus said, "You know the commandments."

The man said, "Master, I have kept them all from my youth."

Jesus looked upon him and loved him. Then he said, "There is just one thing that you lack. Go, sell all that you have and give to the poor, and you will have treasure in heaven. Then come with me."

But when the man heard this he looked sad, for he had great wealth. He went away in sorrow, and Jesus said to His disciples, "Children, how hard it is for those who have wealth to enter the Kingdom of God. It is easier for a camel to go through a needle's eye than for a rich man to enter the Kingdom of God."

They were astonished and said, "Then who can be saved?"

Jesus answered, "With men it is impossible, but not with God, for with God everything is possible."

A Certain Rich Man

NCE a man from the crowd appealed to Jesus and said, "Master, tell my brother to give me my share of the property that belongs to us."

Jesus answered, "Who made me your judge to divide between you?"

Then to the people of the crowd He said, "Take care that you do not become greedy for wealth, for life does not consist in having more things than you need."

Then He told them this story. The land of a certain rich man bore large crops. He thought, "What am I to do since I have no place to store my crops?"

Then he said, "Well, I will do this. I will pull down my barns and build larger ones in which I can store all of my grain and my goods. Then I will have plenty of things laid up for many years to come, and I can take my ease, eat, drink, and be happy."

But God said, "Foolish man! This very night your life is required you, and who will have all the things that you have gathered."

Jesus concluded, "And so it is with the man who lays up

wealth for himself instead of that which in the sight of God is the true wealth. No man can serve two masters. Either he will hate one and love the other, or else he will be loyal to one and untrue to the other. You cannot worship both God and wealth."

The Golden Rule

YOU have heard the saying, 'You shall love your neighbor and hate your enemy.' But I say to you, love your enemies, bless those who curse you, do good to those who hate you, and pray for those who persecute you, that you may become sons of your Father in heaven; for he makes his sun to shine on the wicked and the good alike, and sends rain on both those who do right and those who do wrong. For if you love only those who love you, what reward have you earned?

"Do not even the tax-gatherers as much? And if you show courtesy only to your friends, what more are you doing than others? Do not even the heathen do as much? You must therefore become perfect, even as your heavenly Father is perfect.

"Therefore, whatever you wish that men should do to you, do even so to them."

The return of the Prodigal Son (*Story on page 183*).

Jesus rode into Jerusalem upon the back of the ass, and the people came forth to meet Him. Many spread their clothes on the road while other strewed leafy branches cut from the trees (*Story on page 197*).

Jesus was transfigured with Moses and Elijah on the Mount of Olives, in the presence of Peter, James, and John (*Story on page 204*).

Jesus celebrated the Feast of the Passover with His beloved apostles.
It was the Last Supper He was to have with them (*Story on page 210*).

Casting the First Stone

THE scribes and the Pharisees brought to Jesus a woman who had been caught in a wrong doing, and they said, "Now Moses in the law commanded us that people doing this wrong should be stoned, but what sayest thou?"

Jesus stooped down and wrote with His finger on the ground, as though He did not hear them.

So they asked again, and He stood up and said, "He that is without sin among you, let him first cast a stone at her."

He stooped down again and wrote on the ground, and when He stood up once more, He saw that He was left alone with the woman, for the consciences of the others had disturbed them and they had gone away.

Then Jesus said to the woman, "Where are your accusers? Has no man condemned you?"

She said, "No man, Lord."

And Jesus said to her, "Neither do I condemn you. Go and sin no more."

In the House of the Tax-Gatherer

WHEN Jesus was beside the Sea of Galilee, teaching the crowd, He saw Levi sitting in the house where taxes were collected. Jesus said, "Come with me," and Levi arose and followed Him.

Now while Jesus was eating dinner in Levi's house, many other tax-gatherers and sinners sat down at the same table with Jesus and His disciples.

When they saw this, the scribes and Pharisees said, "What is this? Does Jesus sit down with tax-gatherers and sinners?"

Jesus overheard what they were saying and said, "It is not those who are well, but those who are sick who have need of a healer. I did not come to call the righteous but the sinners to repentance."

At another time Jesus was dining in the house of one of the Pharisees. As He sat down at the table, a wicked woman of the town entered the house, bringing an alabaster jar of perfume. She stood behind Him, weeping, and as her tears began to wet His feet, she wiped them with her hair. Then she opened the jar of perfume and poured it over His feet.

The Pharisee said to himself, "If this man is indeed a

prophet, He ought to know that the woman touching Him is a sinner."

Jesus divined his thoughts and answered them by telling a story. "There was a man," He said, "who owed a certain money-lender five hundred silver pieces, and there was another man who owed the same money-lender fifty pieces of silver. Neither of them was able to pay him anything, so he forgave them the debt. Then," asked Jesus of the Pharisee, "which of these men do you suppose will love him the more?"

"I suppose," said the Pharisee, "that the man who owed him the more will love him the more."

"Yes, you are right," said Jesus, and then he turned to the woman and spoke. He said to Simon, "When I came into this house, you gave me no water for my feet. But she has wet my feet with her tears and wiped them with her hair. You gave me no kiss, but she has not ceased from kissing my feet tenderly. You did not pour oil on my head, but she has poured perfume on my feet. Therefore, I say to you, though her sins are great, they are forgiven, for she has loved me much."

And to the woman He said, "Your sins are forgiven."

The other guests wondered who this stranger was, that He could forgive sins.

But to the woman He said, "Your faith has saved you; Go and be at peace."

The Lost Sheep

HE scribes and the Pharisees were complaining because Jesus let the tax-gatherers and the sinners keep coming to Him. So He answered them by saying:

"What man of you, if he has a hundred sheep and loses one, does not leave the ninety-nine in the wilderness and go and hunt for the lost sheep until he finds it? And when he has found it, he joyfully puts it on his shoulders and when he gets home calls together his friends and says, 'Rejoice with me, for I have found the sheep that I lost.' So I tell you, there will be more joy in heaven over one sinner who is truly sorry and promises to do right than over ninety-nine upright men who have no need to do so.

"Or which of you women, if she has ten silver coins but has lost one, does not light a lamp, sweep the house thoroughly, and search carefully until she finds it? After finding it she calls together her friends and neighbors and says, 'Rejoice with me, for I have found the coin that I lost.' So I tell you, there is rejoicing among the angels over the sinner who is truly sorry and promises to do right."

Christ's Entry into Jerusalem

WHEN Christ was about to leave Bethany, He told two of His disciples to go into a neighboring village, where they would find an ass tied up with her colt by her, which they were to loose, and bring to Him. And if any one tried to prevent them, they were to say that the Lord had need of them.

So they went and found the ass tied up, with her young one, as Jesus had said. And when they were loosing them, some who were standing by asked them why they did so. They answered as they had been bidden, that the Lord had need of them. Then the people immediately let the beasts go, as Jesus had told His disciples that they would do; and they brought the colt and its mother to Him.

In Palestine, where there were very few horses, asses were used for riding upon, even by the greatest people.

So, when the disciples had brought the beasts, they spread their own upper clothing upon the colt's back, and Jesus rode upon him toward Jerusalem. And multitudes came out to meet Him, laying their garments beneath His feet, while others cut down branches from the trees, and strewed them in the way, to show that they received Him as their king.   Then, as the long train passed slowly round the foot of the Mount of Olives, the host of His disciples burst out in shouts of joy: "Blessed be the King that cometh in the name of the Lord: peace in heaven, and glory in the highest." And the vast multitude that went before and followed after took up the cry, "Hosanna! blessed is He that cometh in the name of the Lord!"

Then, as Jesus, with this rejoicing throng, drew near to Jerusalem, and looked upon its walls, and buildings, and its beautiful Temple, all lying before Him, He wept over it. For He thought of the destruction that should come upon it for the wickedness of its people, whom He would have saved, but they would not let Him.

When He came into Jerusalem, the whole city was in a tumult, asking who it was who thus entered it like a king. And the multitudes answered that it was Jesus, the prophet of Nazareth and Galilee, their Messiah!

The chief men of the Jews were vexed that the multitude should acknowledge Christ to be their king.   And it made them all the more eager to lay hold of Him, and kill Him.

Jesus Speaks of Forgiveness

ETER came to Jesus and asked Him, "Master, if my brother do wrong, how many times am I to forgive him? Seven?"

Jesus said, "I tell you, not seven times, but seven times seventy times seven.

"That is why the Kingdom of Heaven is like a king who wished to settle his accounts with his servants. A man was brought before him who owed him ten thousand talents, but since the man was unable to pay it, the master ordered that he be sold, together with his wife and children and all that he had, in payment of the debt. The servant, however, threw himself at his master's feet and begged so hard that the master was moved to pity and forgave him his debt.

"As soon as the servant went out, he met a man who owed him one-sixtieth of a talent. He seized him by the throat and said, 'Pay you what you owe me,' and though the poor fellow begged for more time, he would not grant it and had him imprisoned until he should pay what was due.

"Now when his fellow servants saw what had been done, they were much troubled and came and told their master what had happened. Then the master called him and said, 'What is this? I forgave you the debt I owed you. Should you not show the same mercy to your fellow that I showed to you?'

"In his anger the master turned him over to the jailers until he should pay all that was due."

"So also will my heavenly Father do to you unless each of you sincerely forgives his brother."

The Widow's Mite

ONE day Jesus was sitting opposite the Temple where He could see the people coming to put in their money. Many rich men came and put in large sums, but after a time a poor woman came and dropped in two small coins which were worth less than a penny.

Observing this Jesus called to His disciples and said to them, "I tell you, this poor widow has given more than all the rest who have put their money into the treasury; for they have given out of their plenty, but she, out of her poverty, has given all that she has, even that which she needed to keep her alive."

The Warning to the Disciples

S Jesus went out of the Temple, one of His disciples said, "What a beautiful building it is."

Jesus answered, "This Temple, made by man's hands, shall soon be destroyed. But another will soon arise, made without hands."

Then He went up on the Mount of Olives opposite the Temple, and Peter and James and John and Andrew went with Him. They said, "Tell us, when shall all these things happen, and what is the sign that they are about to happen."

Jesus answered them and said, "No one knows the day or the hour when this will happen, not the angels in heaven, nor the Son, but only the Father."

Then He told them a story about ten maidens who took their torches in their hand and went out to meet the bridegroom. Five of them were foolish and five were wise. The foolish ones took only their torches and no oil with them. But the wise ones took oil in another vessel to fill their torches. It happened that the bridegroom was delayed, and it was midnight before the cry arose that he was coming. The foolish virgins saw that their torches were almost burned out, and they begged the wise ones for more oil, but the wise maidens answered that they did not have enough for all of them. So while the foolish ones went out to buy oil, the bridegroom came in and the door was locked. Later when the foolish virgins came back with their filled lamps to the marriage feast, the door was shut and the bridegroom refused to open it, for he said he did not know who they were.

Therefore Jesus bade the apostles take a lesson and be continually on watch, for no one would know the day nor the hour when the Kingdom of God would come.

Jesus Talks to Elijah and Moses

ONCE Jesus took Peter, James, and John up on a high mountain where they were alone. In their presence, he was transfigured. His clothes glistened with a dazzling whiteness, such as no earthly bleaching could give them. As the disciples looked, there appeared Elijah and Moses, who talked with Jesus.

Then Peter said, "Master, it is fortunate that we are here. Let us make three tabernacles, one for you, one for Moses, and one for Elijah."

Just then a cloud came and overshadowed them, and he heard a voice from the cloud say, "This is my Beloved Son; give heed to him."

Then they came down from the mountain, and Jesus commanded them to tell no one of what they had seen and heard until after He had risen from the dead.

Bartimaeus the Beggar

JESUS was leaving Jericho with His disciples followed by a large crowd, when He came to a road where a blind beggar sat. When the man heard that it was Jesus of Nazareth, he cried out, "Jesus, son of David, have pity on me!"

Many of the people tried to restrain him, saying, "Keep still," but he only cried out more loudly than before.

Jesus stopped and said, "Let him come to me."

Then the blind man threw off his cloak and came and stood before Jesus, and Jesus said, "What do you want me to do for you?"

The blind man answered, "Master, let me receive my sight."

Then Jesus said, "Go your way, your faith has healed you."

At once he received his sight and followed Jesus along the road.

The Story of Lazarus

AT the foot of the Mount of Olives, about two miles from Jerusalem, in the town of Bethany lived some friends of Jesus, a man named Lazarus, and his sisters Mary and Martha.

So now, as Jesus came near Bethany, Mary and Martha sent a message to Him saying that Lazarus was sick. When Jesus heard that, He said that Lazarus' illness was not unto death, but was for the glory of God, that the son of God might be glorified thereby.

After two days had gone by, while Jesus still remained in the same place, He said to His disciples, "Let us go into Judea again."

The disciples sought to prevent His going, for they reminded Him that the Jews had sought to stone Him before and they said, "Why goest thou thither again?"

He said, "Our friend Lazarus sleepeth; but I go that I may awake him out of sleep."

The disciples answered, "Lord, if he sleep, he shall do well."

Jesus saw that they did not know what He meant; so He spoke plainly and said, "Lazarus is dead."

When Jesus came to Bethany, He found that Lazarus had been buried for four days. As soon as she heard that He was coming, Martha went to meet Him, but Mary sat still in the house.

Martha said to Jesus, "Lord, if Thou hadst been here, my brother had not died. But I know, that, even now, whatever Thou wilt ask of God, God will give it to Thee."

Jesus said to her, "Thy brother shall rise again."

And He said, "I am the resurrection, and the life; he that believeth in me, though he were dead, yet shall he live."

And Martha believed, and went to call Mary and tell her that The Master had come and was asking for her.

All the Jews who were mourning with Mary and Martha for Lazarus saw her rise, and they thought that she was going to his grave to weep for him. So they followed her to comfort her if they could.

When Mary came to where Jesus was waiting for her, she fell down at His feet and said, "Lord, if thou hadst been here, my brother had not died."

When Jesus saw her weeping, and the Jews who were with her weeping also, He was greatly troubled.

He said, "Where have you laid him?"

They led Him to the burial place, and when He saw it, Jesus wept. The grave was a cave, with a stone before it.

Jesus said, "Take away the stone."

Martha objected at first, saying that Lazarus had been dead four days, but Jesus reproached her and reminded her that He had said that if she believed, she should see the glory

Lazarus came forth from the tomb.

of God. The stone was rolled away, and Jesus, after a prayer
to His Father in Heaven, stepped to the mouth of the cave
and cried, in a loud voice, "Lazarus, come forth."

Lazarus came forth, still in his burial garments, and Jesus
spoke to the people and asked them to unloose him and let
him go.

Six days before the Passover, Jesus came again to Bethany,
where Lazarus lived. There they made Him a supper and
Martha served. Lazarus sat at the table. And as they sat
there eating, Mary came with a pound of ointment of spike-
nard, which was very costly, and anointed His feet and wiped
them with her hair.

A VIEW OF THE SEA OF GALILEE
AT SUNDOWN

THE STORY OF THE PICTURE
(on inside pages)

PETER FINDS THE TAX MONEY
(Matt. 17: 24-27)

Peter has just found, in the mouth of a fish, the money demanded by the tax collectors. He calls out excitedly as he runs towards Jesus, waving the coin so that all may see. The Roman tax collectors are stunned with amazement as they witness the fulfillment of Christ's command to Peter, ". . . Take up the fish that first cometh up; and when thou hast opened his mouth, thou shalt find a piece of money: that take, and give unto them for me and thee." Soldier and disciple are electrified by the event and do not fully comprehend that which has taken place before their eyes. Jesus, alone, remains understandingly calm and serene.

SITE OF THE ANCIENT TEMPLE, JERUSALEM

Then said one of the disciples, Judas Iscariot, "Why was not this ointment sold for three hundred pence, and the money given to the poor?"

Now, he was not so greatly concerned with the poor, but he had the bag of money for the poor and was interested in what it contained.

But Jesus answered, "Why do you trouble the woman? She hath wrought a good work upon me. The poor you will always have with you, but you will not always have me with you."

Many people came from Jerusalem, not only to see Him, but Lazarus also. The chief priests and rulers of the Jews knew that Christ was at Bethany; and they plotted to put Lazarus to death as well as Christ, because the miracle that had been performed on him caused many to believe Jesus to be the Son of God.

The Last Supper

JESUS went back again to Bethany in the evening, returning to Jerusalem the next day to teach the people, and work miracles for their good. And this He did every day till His enemies seized Him, in order to put Him to death.

The chief priests and rulers of the Jews were planning among themselves how they might best take Jesus, when Judas Iscariot, one of the twelve disciples, went to them, and asked what they would give him if he would deliver up Jesus to them. They agreed to give him thirty pieces of silver—that is, about five pounds of our money! And for this Judas was willing to betray his Master, as soon as he could find a convenient opportunity of doing it.

Now, when the Feast of the Passover was to be kept, the twelve disciples asked Jesus where they should prepare it. At this feast, the Jews solemnly ate together of a lamb, and bread made without leaven (or ferment), in memory of their deliverance out of the land of Egypt.

Jesus told His disciples to go into the city, where they would meet a man carrying a vessel of water. They were to follow this man, and ask the master of the house into which he entered to show them a room where they might eat the Passover. So they went, and found it as Jesus had said; and they made ready the Passover.

In the evening Jesus came to the house, and sat down to supper with the twelve disciples. And He told them how earnestly He had longed to eat that Passover with them, for it was the last that He should keep. Then, as they were eating, He said that one of them should betray Him to His enemies. They were very sorrowful when they heard this, each one asking anxiously if it should be he. Even Judas ventured to ask, as the others did, "Is it I?" As if his Lord did not know all his treachery! And Jesus told him it was he.

Then Jesus took bread, and, after He had given thanks to God, He brake it and gave it to the disciples, telling them that represented His body about to be slain for them. And He bade them eat it in remembrance of Him. He then took a cup of wine, and having given thanks, bade them all drink of it; for that wine represented His blood which was about to be shed, in order that the sins of all human beings might be forgiven.

For thirty pieces of silver, Judas Iscariot, one of the disciples, agreed to deliver up Jesus to the rulers.

Christr Washing His Disciples' Feet

WHEN He rose from supper, Jesus put off His upper garment, which was a loose, flowing robe, such as is worn in the East. Then, taking a towel, He poured water into a basin, and began to wash the feet of His disciples, wiping them with the towel.

When He came to wash the feet of Peter, Peter would have prevented Him; for he was ashamed that his Lord should render him so mean a service. Jesus answered that He would presently tell him why He did it; and at last Peter suffered Him to wash his feet.

Then, when our Lord had put on His garment, and sat down with them again, He asked the disciples if they knew why He had washed their feet. And He went on to tell them that He had done it in order to teach them that as He, whom they called Master and Lord, and who indeed was so, had not thought it beneath Him to act as though He were their servant, they ought to be willing to serve each other in any way, however mean.

Then Jesus comforted His disciples, who were very sorrowful, because He had said He was about to die. He bade them not let their hearts be troubled or afraid, for He was going to prepare a place for them in His Father's house in heaven. And He promised that, when He was gone up into heaven, He would send to them God's Holy Spirit, who should be with them always, to comfort and teach them, and bring to their minds all that He had taught them while He was Himself with them. And again He bade them not let their hearts be troubled. And many other loving words He said to them; and He prayed for them, and for all who should afterward believe in Him as the Savior of the world.

Then, when they had sung a hymn, they went out in the clear moonlight night, over the brook Cedron, to the Mount of Olives. And as they walked along, Jesus told His disciples that they would all forsake Him when His enemies had seized Him, as they were just about to do. Peter indignantly denied that he would forsake his Master: though all the others might do so, he would never leave Him. Christ answering, told him that that very night, even before the cock should crow twice, he would thrice deny that he knew any thing of Jesus. But Peter warmly replied that, though he were to die with his Master, he would never deny Him. And so said all the rest of the disciples.

Judas Betraying With a Kiss

WHEN they all went into a garden called Gethsemane; and Jesus, taking with Him Peter, James, and John, bade the rest of the disciples stay there, while He went a little farther and prayed.

And when He was alone with the three, they saw that, though He had been speaking such loving, comforting words to them, He was Himself overwhelmed with sorrow. And He said to them that His soul was exceedingly sorrowful, even unto death. Then telling them to stay with Him while He prayed, He went to a little distance, and, bending down to the very ground in His agony, He prayed that if it were possible God would spare Him the bitter sufferings which He must bear in order to save the world saying, "Father, with Thee all things are possible. Take away this cup of agony from me. Yet not my will, but Thy will be done."

As He prayed, His agony of mind was so great that the blood forced itself through His veins, falling in great drops to the ground; and God, in His pity, sent an angel to strengthen Him.

When He came back, He found the disciples asleep; and

He said to Peter, "Simon, are you asleep? Could you not watch for one hour? Watch and pray that you may overcome temptation. The spirit indeed is willing, but the body is weak."

Again He went away and prayed the same prayer. And when He returned, again He found them asleep, for they were very drowsy; and they did not know what to say to Him.

Then He came the third time and said, "Sleep on now and take your rest. It is enough; the hour has come; already the Son of Man has been betrayed into the hands of wicked men. Rise, let us go; for here is the one who betrayed me."

While Jesus was yet speaking, an unruly multitude, carrying lanterns and torches, and armed with swords, clubs, and other weapons, burst into the garden, with Judas at their head. Jesus went forward to meet them, asking whom they sought. They said, "Jesus of Nazareth." Jesus answered, "I am He." And when He said this, they drew back and fell to the ground as though they had been dead.

Now Judas had told the people who came with him that the man whom he should kiss was He whom they were to take. So he stepped up to Jesus, and calling Him "Master!" kissed Him. Then Peter, seeing Jesus seized by these ruffians, drew his sword to defend his Master; and, striking one of the servants of the high-priest, cut off his ear. But Jesus bade him sheathe his sword again; for if it were His will to escape, God would send legions of angels to protect Him. And He stretched out His hand, touched the man's ear, and it was whole again.

Then all His disciples forsook Him and fled, leaving Jesus alone in the hands of His enemies!

One young man, however, followed Him with only a linen sheet thrown about him; but when the men tried to seize him, he left the linen sheet and fled away naked.

The Crown of Thorns

THE high-priest and the rulers of the Jews, before whom Jesus was brought, were determined to put Him to death. But as He had never done any thing wrong, it was hard work to find a pretense for doing so.

At length the high-priest solemnly bade Jesus tell them whether He was indeed the Christ, the Son of God. Jesus answered that He was the Christ; and that at the end of the world they should see Him coming in the clouds of heaven, to judge all men. Then the high-priest rent his clothes (which was the way in which the Jews expressed grief and horror); and those who were with him exclaimed, that for Jesus to call Himself the Son of God was such wickedness that He ought to be put to death.

Then his guards fell upon Jesus, and ill-treated Him in every possible way. They spat upon Him, they smote Him; and when they had blindfolded Him, they struck Him on the face, bidding Him, as He was a prophet, to tell them who it was that had struck Him. And many other cruelties they committed against Him.

Meanwhile Peter, who had turned back again to see what

became of his Master, was waiting outside among the officers and servants of the palace. And as he stood warming himself by the fire, a maid-servant, looking earnestly at Peter, said that he was one who had been with Jesus of Nazareth. But Peter, declaring that he did not know Jesus, went away to another part of the palace. And immediately the cock crew. Then another servant said, "This fellow also was with Jesus of Nazareth." And again Peter denied that he knew anything of Him. In about an hour after, some of those who were standing about said that Peter was certainly one of Christ's disciples, because he came from Galilee, where Jesus lived. Then Peter swore that he knew nothing of Jesus. And immediately the cock crew the second time. Then Peter remembered that Jesus had told him that before the cock should crow twice, he would deny Him thrice. And he went out, and wept bitterly.

After the chief priests and rulers had condemned Jesus, they took Him before Pontius Pilate, the Roman governor. Pilate ordered Jesus to be scourged; and then he gave Him into the hands of the soldiers, who platted a crown of thorns, and put it on His head, clothed Him in a purple robe, and then mocked Him, pretending to do Him reverence as the King of the Jews!

Christen Bearing His Cross

THEN Judas, who had betrayed Jesus, repented of his wickedness. And he brought back to the chief priests the money they had given him; and, exclaiming that he had sinned in betraying an innocent person, went out, and hanged himself.

Pilate had yielded to the clamor of the Jews when he gave up Jesus to the soldiers. But he soon perceived that Jesus was innocent of the evil deeds laid to His charge, and he was very anxious to save Him. So, when the soldiers had scourged Him, Jesus was brought out, faint, and wearing the crown and purple robe with which He had been mocked. And Pilate said to the people, "Behold the man!" hoping they would pity Jesus and let him release Him. But they only cried out, "Crucify Him, crucify Him!" Pilate indignantly bade them crucify Him themselves, for he found no fault in Him. Then the Jews, seeing how bent Pilate was on saving Jesus, told him that if he let Jesus go he would be guilty of treason to the Roman emperor, because Christ had called Himself a king. Pilate was afraid when he heard this. Still he tried again and again to persuade them to let him release

Jesus; and as it was the custom that, at the Feast of the Passover, some one criminal, whom they chose, should be set at liberty, he wanted them to let Jesus be this one. But they chose a robber, named Barabbas, instead. And when Pilate asked them what he must then do with Jesus, they cried out, as before, "Let Him be crucified."

Then Pilate, finding that nothing but the death of Jesus would satisfy the Jews, at length shamefully gave way to them. But before he delivered Jesus to the soldiers to be crucified, he took water, and washing his hands before the multitude, as was the custom when any one wished to show his innocence of any crime, he told them that he was innocent of the death of that just person; they must bear the blame of it.

Then the soldiers took Jesus; and after they had grievously insulted Him, they led Him away to crucify Him, compelling Him Himself to carry the cross upon which He was to be put to death. But Jesus was so faint and worn out with the cruel treatment which He had received that He could not carry the heavy cross which they had laid upon Him. So they seized a countryman whom they met, and made him bear it after Jesus.

And great numbers followed Jesus, weeping and lamenting for Him.

The Crucifixion

WHEN they were come to a rising ground, named Calvary, they crucified Jesus there, along with two thieves, one on each side of Him. Upon the cross was written, "This is Jesus of Nazareth, the King of the Jews." And the soldiers, and many of the people who stood looking on, mocked Him, bidding Him save Himself, and come down from the cross, if He were indeed the Son of God. But Jesus prayed for His tormentors, saying, "Father, forgive them; they know not what they do."

One of the thieves also that were crucified with Him spoke insultingly to Jesus. But the other thief rebuked his companion, saying that they were justly punished for their ill deeds, while Jesus had done nothing amiss. Then he prayed Jesus to remember him when He entered into His kingdom. And Jesus said unto him, "To-day shalt thou be with me in Paradise."

Then, though it was midday, it became dark over the whole land of Judea. And amid the darkness Jesus cried with a loud voice, "My God, my God, why hast Thou forsaken me?" Some who stood there, pitying Him, ran and filled a sponge with wine, and putting it on a reed in order to reach His lips, gave Him drink. Then, when He had drunk, He again cried out with a loud voice, "It is finished!" His head sank down, and He died.

And immediately a great earthquake shook the ground, tearing the rocks in pieces, so that many graves were opened. And the bodies of holy people, who had been laid in them, came to life again after Christ's resurrection, and went into Jerusalem, where they were seen by many.

It was the custom of the Romans to break the legs of those who had been crucified, in order that they might die more speedily. But when the soldiers came to do this, they found Christ was already dead. So they did not break His legs, but one of them pierced His side with a spear, and blood and water flowed from the wound.

Then one of the Jewish rulers, named Joseph, came to Pilate, and begged that he might have the body of Jesus to bury it. Pilate gave him leave to have it. So he took Jesus down from the cross, wrapped Him in fine linen, and when he had laid Him in his own new tomb, which was cut in the rock, he closed it with a large stone.

Wearing the crown of thorns and carrying His heavy burden, Jesus was led to Golgotha where He was crucified.

While Jesus prayed, the apostles slept (*Story on page 215*).

Jesus was bound and taken before Pontius Pilate (*Story on page 216*).

Pilate, the Roman Governor, turned Jesus over to the soldiers who led Him away to be crucified (*Story on page 220*).

He died for us (*Story on page 223*).

Christave Appears to Mary

THEN the chief priests came to Pilate. And they said to him that as Jesus before His death had told the people that in three days after He should rise from the dead and be alive again, it would be better that a guard should be placed over His tomb, lest His disciples should steal the body by night, and then say that He was risen from the dead. So Pilate told them to take a guard of Roman soldiers; and they placed a seal on the stone over the tomb, that they might make sure that no one had attempted to remove it.

Very early in the morning of the first day of the week, Mary Magdalene, and Mary the wife of Cleophas, came to the tomb, that they might, according to the custom in the East, wrap up the body of Christ with spices and gums, which would prevent its decay. As they went, they wondered who would roll away for them the great stone that closed the tomb. But when they reached the place, the stone was already rolled away; and an angel, in bright shining garments, sat there, who bade them not be afraid, for he knew that they sought Jesus of Nazareth, who was risen from the dead. And he said to the women that they must go and tell the disciples, and Peter, that they would find their Lord in Galilee, as before His death He had told them they should do.

Then the women went away quickly, trembling with fear and joy, to tell the disciples. Peter and John ran at once to the tomb, to see if what they had heard was indeed true; and finding it empty, returned again to their own homes, for they scarcely understood what had been said to them about Christ rising from the dead.

But Mary Magdalene, who was with them, stayed behind at the tomb, weeping. And as she wept some one stood by her, and asked her why she wept, and whom it was that she was seeking. She, supposing him to be the gardener, begged him, if he had taken away the body of Jesus, to tell her where he had laid it, that she might take it away. Jesus (for it was He Himself) said to her, "Mary!" She instantly knew His voice, and answering, "Master!" clung to His feet for very joy, worshiping Him.

Then Jesus told her to go and tell His disciples that He was risen from the dead, and that He should very soon ascend to heaven to His Father and theirs.

So she went and told the disciples that she had seen Jesus. But they could not believe her.

The Ascension

JESUS next appeared to two of the disciples as they were going from Jerusalem to a village called Emmaus, and were sorrowfully talking about the death of their Master.

There, as they sat at supper, He took bread, and blessing it, gave it to them. Then they knew their Lord; and when He vanished out of their sight, they hastened back again to Jerusalem to tell the other disciples that Jesus was indeed risen from the dead, for they had seen Him.

While they were telling what they had seen, Jesus Himself stood among them, and blessed them. And they were afraid, thinking they had seen a spirit. But He bade them touch Him, that they might know it was not a spirit that they saw, but His own body. And He showed them, on His hands and His side, the marks of the cruel wounds that He had received. Then, as they still, for very joy, scarcely believed it was He, He took some broiled fish and a piece of honeycomb, and ate it before them, in order to convince them that it was indeed Himself in His own body. Then the disciples were glad when they felt sure it was Jesus Himself who was with them.

After this, Peter, and some other of the disciples, went fishing on the Sea of Tiberias, in Galilee. They caught nothing that night; but at daybreak they saw some one standing on the shore, who asked them kindly if they had any fish. They said no. He bade them cast their net on the right side of the boat; and when they had done so, they caught so many fishes that they could not draw the net to land. Then John exclaimed that it was the Lord! Peter, hearing this, immediately threw on his fisher's coat, and sprang into the water, that he might go to his Master. Then, when they were all come to land, Jesus bade them come and dine; for He had a fire there, on which fish was broiling; and bread also.

And they all now knew that Jesus, who had been crucified, and who had risen from the dead, was their Lord and God!

Vast numbers of people saw Jesus after His resurrection from the dead. Then, at the end of forty days, He went out to Bethany with the eleven apostles. There He gave them His last blessing; and while He was blessing them, He ascended from the earth, and was taken up into heaven.

The Lame Man Cured by Peter

ONE day as Peter and John walked through the Beautiful Gate of the magnificent Temple at Jerusalem, at the hour of prayer, they noticed a lame man sitting there. This man had been lame from birth, and it was the custom of his friends to carry him to the gate of the Temple so that he might remain there throughout the day and beg alms of those who were entering to worship the Lord.

The poor lame man saw Peter and John approaching and he begged for some small gift.

Peter, however, fastened his eyes upon the man, and said, "Look on us!"

The man immediately gave heed to them, expecting that they were about to give him something.

But Peter said, "Silver and gold have I none; but such as I have give I thee. In the name of Jesus Christ of Nazareth rise up and walk!"

Then Peter held forth his hand and took the lame man by the right hand, and lifted him up. Immediately the lame man's feet and ankle bones became well and strong! He leaped up and stood, and found that he could walk. He entered the temple with Peter and John, and in his excitement and joy he leaped about, all the while praising God.

All the people saw this man walking and praising God, and they were filled with wonder and amazement at this miracle that had taken place, for they knew that it was the same man they had seen sitting at the Beautiful Gate of the Temple asking alms.

The lame man, who was now perfectly well, held on to Peter and John, while all the people collected together and ran toward them, gathering at the Porch of Solomon, wondering and questioning how this miracle had been done.

When Peter saw how they had all come together, he knew that this was a good opportunity to tell them of the power of the Lord Jesus Christ. Therefore he spoke to them, saying, "Ye men of Israel, why marvel ye at this? Or why look ye so earnestly on us, as though by our own power or holiness we had made this man to walk?

"The God of Abraham, and of Isaac, and of Jacob, the God of our fathers, hath glorified His Son Jesus; whom ye delivered up, and denied Him in the presence of Pilate, when he was determined to let Him go. But ye denied the Holy One and the Just, and desired a murderer to be granted unto you; and killed the Prince of life, whom God hath raised from the dead; whereof we are witnesses."

Peter was, of course, referring to Barabbas, the thief who had been freed at the request of the people, when Pilate had wanted Jesus to be set free instead.

Then Peter went on preaching, and pointing out that

faith in the Lord Jesus had made the lame man strong again.

Repent ye therefore," cried Peter, "and be converted, that your sins may be blotted out." Peter explained to the people that only in this way would they some day come into the presence of God, for their belief in Jesus Christ would be the means of their being accepted by the Almighty Father, and thus receiving eternal life.

Then Peter reminded the multitude that was gathered there listening to him of what Moses had said to their forefathers, of a prophet whom the Lord would raise before them, and whose teachings they should hear in all things, and pay heed to whatever He told them.

Peter became even more emphatic, when he reminded them that Moses had also said, "And it shall come to pass, that every soul, which will not hear that prophet, shall be destroyed from among the people." Thus Moses had warned the people many years before the birth of Christ.

Then Peter went on preaching, saying, "Yea, and all the prophets from Samuel and those that follow after, as many as have spoken, have likewise foretold of these days. Ye are the children of the prophets, and of the covenant which God made with our fathers, saying unto Abraham, 'And in thy seed shall all the kindreds of the earth be blessed.' Unto you first God, having raised up His Son Jesus, sent Him to bless you, in turning away every one of you from his iniquities."

Many of the people who heard the forceful words of Peter believed what he had said, and they began to have faith in the Lord Jesus Christ and the eternal life He offered to those who believed in Him. Peter's eloquence convinced them that Jesus Christ was the Savior of the world, and His great power in performing miracles through His Apostles was a visible evidence of His great power. More and more people came to believe in Him and follow His teachings, happy to think that their faith in Jesus would bring life everlasting to them.

The Death of Ananias

NOW when Peter and John told the people that Jesus whom they had crucified was the Savior of the world, the chief priests and rulers of the Jews were so angry that they laid hold of the apostles and shut them up in prison.

The next day, being brought before a number of the chief people, they were asked by what means they had cured the lame man. Peter told them that it was Jesus whom the Jews had crucified, and whom God had raised from the dead, who had done this miracle. Then they commanded the apostles not to tell the people any more that Jesus was the Savior of the world, threatening to punish them if they did so. But Peter answered that God Himself had bidden them tell this to every one, so they must do it.

Many thousands of the people believed what the apostles told them of Jesus. And they were so kind and loving to each other, that those of them who were rich sold their lands and houses, and brought the money to the apostles, that they might give to the poor.

But there was a man named Ananias, who, when he had

sold his land, brought to the apostles only a part of the price of it, pretending that it was the whole. Then Peter asked him how it was that he had let Satan lead him to tell a lie about this money. The money was his own, and he might have kept the whole of it, instead of a part, if he had wished. But to tell a lie about it was a grievous sin against God.

Then, when Ananias heard Peter say this, he fell down and died. And they took up his dead body, carried it out, and buried him.

About three hours afterward, Sapphira, the wife of Ananias, came in, not knowing what had happened. And Peter asked her whether the money that Ananias had brought to the apostles was all that they had received for the land. She answered, Yes, it was. Then Peter asked her how it was that both she and her husband had agreed to tell a lie, in order to deceive them. And he told her that those who had just buried her husband were at the door, and they would also carry her out and bury her. Then she immediately fell down, and died at Peter's feet. And the young men carried her out, and buried her by her husband.

And all the disciples were afraid when they saw how God had punished Ananias and Sapphira for telling lies.

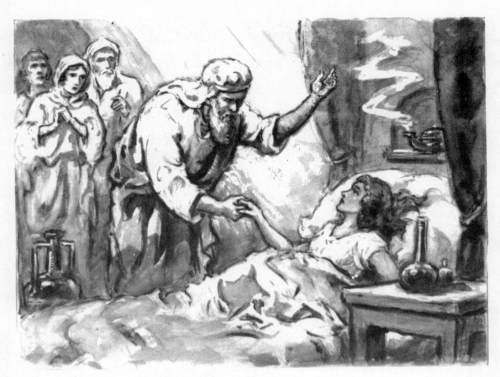

Peter said, "Arise, Dorcas!"

Peter Restores Tabitha to Life

T JOPPA there was a certain disciple named Tabitha, which also means Dorcas. This woman did many good deeds and helped the poor and the needy.

While Peter was in Lydda, which is near Joppa, the disciples sent him word to come to her; for she had fallen sick and died.

Peter went to the house, and they led him to an upper

chamber where she was lying. All around her the widows stood weeping, showing the cloaks and garments which she had made before her death.

Peter asked them all to go out of the room, and then he knelt down beside the couch and prayed. Then he turned towards the body and said, "Tabitha, arise."

She opened her eyes, and when she saw Peter, she sat up. And he gave her his hand and lifted her up, and when he had called the disciples and the widows, he presented her to them alive.

The story of this deed became known through Joppa, and because of it many people came to believe in the Lord.

Peter now decided to remain in Joppa for awhile. He went to live in the house of a man named Simon, who was a tanner. This meant that he worked on the skins of dead animals and made them into leather. Tanners were not looked upon favorably by the Jews, who scorned work of this sort. Peter, however, did not feel this way, for he had seen how Jesus had befriended all kinds of people, whether rich or poor, saints or sinners, old or young alike. Jesus had turned those who were misled into the right paths, and had even chosen men who were ordinarily scorned by the Jews to be His beloved disciples. Peter, therefore, knew that he was doing the right thing by being friendly to any man who needed the help of Jesus, such as tax-collectors, tanners, Gentiles and even Samaritans.

One day while Peter was still at Joppa, God sent a vision to him, in which he was to understand that any creature which had been made by God and had been cleansed by Him was good for man to eat. Therefore, Peter was allowed to eat many foods that he had always considered unclean. God also taught Peter in the vision that he should not consider any one race of man better than another.

Then Peter said, "Of a truth I perceive that God is no respecter of persons: but in every nation he that feareth Him, and worketh righteousness, is accepted with Him."

Peter now understood that all men, whether Jews or Gentiles, were equal in the sight of God.

The Death of Stephen

HE apostles did so many miracles in the name of Jesus of Nazareth, that the chief priests again shut them up in prison.

But at night the angel of the Lord came, and opening the prison-doors, brought out the apostles, and bade them teach, in the Temple itself, that Jesus Christ was the Savior of all men. So, early in the morning, they went into the Temple, and taught the people about Jesus.

Then, when the chief priests and rulers were met together, they ordered the apostles to be brought before them. But when the officers went to the prison to fetch them, they found that they were not there. So they returned, saying that they had found the prison shut up safely, and the keepers watching outside as usual; but when they opened the doors, the prisoners were gone. While they were all wondering at this, some one came in to tell them that the prisoners, whom they could not find, were in the Temple teaching the people. Then the chief priests sent the captain of the guard to bring the apostles to them; and after they had beaten them, they let them go, forbidding them to speak any more to the people about Jesus.

Among the number of the disciples at this time was a man named Stephen, who was one of those who had been chosen to take care of the poor. He was a very good man, and did great wonders and miracles. But some of the Jews were so angry with Stephen that they laid hold of him, dragged him before the rulers, and there accused him of having spoken wickedly of Moses, and even of God Himself.

Then, out of those books that Moses and others of their own prophets had written, Stephen showed how wickedly the Jews had acted, and how grievously they had sinned against God in killing those whom He had sent to teach them; and at last, in having put to death even God's own Son. And when he had spoken to them in this way, he looked up steadfastly to heaven, and saw the glory of God, and Jesus standing on His right hand. And he told the people that he saw the heavens opened, and the Son of Man, that is, Jesus Christ, standing at the right hand of God.

Then they cried out against him, hurried him out of the city, and put him cruelly to death by stoning. And as they stoned him, he exclaimed, "Lord Jesus, receive my spirit." And praying God to forgive his murderers, he died as though he had been falling asleep.

Conversion of Saul

MONG those who put Stephen to death was a young man named Saul. He was a bitter persecutor of those who believed in Jesus; and the high-priest sent him to Damascus, to bring any Christians whom he found there back with him to Jerusalem.

Damascus is a city in Syria, more than a hundred miles from Jerusalem. And when Saul had been traveling some days, as he came near the city, suddenly there shone round him a light of such dazzling brightness that he fell, bewildered, to the ground. Amid the light a glorious form was seen, and he heard a voice, saying to him, "Saul, Saul, why persecutest thou me?"

Then Saul asked, "Who art thou, Lord?"

And the voice answered, "I am Jesus of Nazareth, whom thou persecutest."

Then Saul, amazed and trembling, asked what he must do. And the Lord bade him arise, and go to Damascus, and there it should be told him what he must do.

Now the men who were traveling with Saul stood by, speechless with astonishment and fear; for they saw the light,

JOSEPH'S GATEWAY, CAVE OF MACHPELAH,
HEBRON

THE STORY OF THE PICTURE
(on inside pages)

JOHN SEES A NEW HEAVEN AND A NEW EARTH
(Rev. 21: 2-4)

John is on the rocky and desolate Isle of Patmos. In striking contrast to his surroundings, he foresees the glorious reality of "a new heaven and a new earth." His vision of the holy city is revealed in sudden glory before his startled eyes. The supreme moment of his life has come. He beholds the image of a divine city, bathed in celestial light, and "coming down from God out of heaven, prepared as a bride adorned for her husband." John lies among the rough rocks which have torn his clothing and bruised his body, but his thoughts are exalted high above his bleak surroundings to the New Jerusalem . . . the promise and fulfillment for all men.

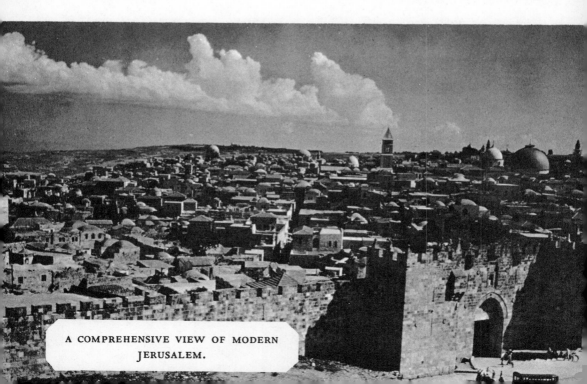

A COMPREHENSIVE VIEW OF MODERN JERUSALEM.

and heard the awful voice, though they did not see Him whom Saul saw.

Then Saul arose from the earth. But he was quite blinded by the dazzling light, so that his followers had to lead him till they reached Damascus. There he remained blind for three days, and in such distress of mind for his wickedness in persecuting the disciples that he could neither eat nor drink.

Now there was at Damascus a disciple named Ananias, to whom the Lord spoke in a dream, bidding him go to a certain street in the city, where he would find Saul of Tarsus, who was repenting of his past misdeeds. Ananias was afraid to go, for he knew how cruelly Saul had treated the Christians at Jerusalem, and also that he was come to Damascus on purpose to seize the Christians there. But the Lord bade him not fear to go, because He had chosen Saul to be one of His apostles to teach the Gentiles—that is, those who were not Jews—that Jesus was their Savior.

Then Ananias went, and, putting his hands upon Saul, told him that the Lord Jesus, whom he had seen on his journey, had sent him to cure him of his blindness, and that he might receive God's Holy Spirit.

And immediately Saul's sight was restored to him. And when he had been baptized, he taught in the synagogue that Jesus Christ was the Son of God, who had died to save all men.

Peter Before Cornelius

ONCE Peter stayed for a long time at Joppa, in the house of Simon, a tanner.

The captain of the Italian guard, a man named Cornelius, lived in Caesarea. He was a good man, and all of his household worshiped God. He gave gifts to the poor and served God in all ways.

One afternoon, about three o'clock, a vision came to Cornelius. He saw an angel coming and saying to him, " Cornelius."

Although he was afraid, Cornelius looked straight at the angel and said, "What is it, Lord?"

The angel answered, "Your prayers and gifts to the poor are pleasing to God. Now send to Joppa and bring a certain Simon, who is also called Peter. You will find him in the house of a tanner named Simon, whose house is by the seaside."

When the vision disappeared, Cornelius called two of his servants and a certain trusted soldier. He explained to them what had happened, and sent them to Joppa.

They reached Joppa about noon, just as Peter had gone

Peter was brought before Cornelius, the Roman officer, in accordance with God's command.

up to the housetop to pray. They were at the gate calling out to inquire whether Simon, whose other name was Peter, was inside, and he heard them, and knew that they were looking for him. But the Spirit told him not to be afraid, so he went down at once and asked them what they desired.

They answered, explaining their mission, and Peter agreed to go with them. The next morning they started out, and when they reached Caesarea, Cornelius was waiting for them. When he saw Peter, he fell down on his knees to worship him. Peter stopped him saying, "I am only a man like you."

Then Cornelius told him how the angel had commanded him to send for Peter, and he concluded, "Now we are all here in the presence of God, to listen to whatever God has commanded you to say."

Peter said, "I see, truly, that God shows no partiality; but in every nation, the man who reveres Him, and does what is right, is pleasing to Him."

Then all those who heard Peter began to shout and praise the Lord, and the Jewish disciples who came with Peter were amazed, because the gift of the Holy Spirit was poured out on those who were not Jews.

Then Peter said, "Can any one refuse to baptize those who, as well as we, have received the Holy Spirit?"

And he commanded that they be baptized in the name of Jesus Christ.

Peter Delivered Out of Prison

HEROD AGRIPPA, king of Judea, persecuted the Christians. James, the brother of John, he beheaded; and then he shut up Peter in prison, intending to put him to death also.

The disciples were greatly afflicted at this, and prayed very earnestly to God that He would deliver Peter out of the power of the wicked king.

Now Peter was one night sleeping in his prison, between two soldiers, to whom he was chained by each hand, when, suddenly, a bright light shone around, and an angel of the Lord stood by him, and bade him rise quickly, put on his clothing and his shoes, and follow him. As the angel spoke, Peter's chains fell off; and he rose, clothed himself, and followed the angel, thinking it was all a dream. The prison-doors were closely guarded as usual; but they passed on, without any one seeing them, till they reached the great iron gate. This opened to them of itself; and they went out through it, and along a certain street, where the angel left Peter.

Then, when he was at last convinced that he was really

brought out of prison, Peter knew that it was God Himself who had sent an angel to deliver him from the cruelty of King Herod and the Jews. And he went on to the house of Mary, one of the disciples, where many of his friends were praying for him. When he knocked at the gate, a young woman, named Rhoda, came to see who it was. And when she heard Peter's voice, she was so glad, that for very joy she forgot to open the gate, but ran into the house instead to tell them that Peter was standing there. They told her she must be mad to suppose such a thing, for they knew how Peter had been chained in prison. But she declared it was certainly he. And as he kept knocking, they at last opened the door, and then they found that it was indeed Peter himself.

Then Peter told them how God had sent an angel to deliver him out of prison; and bidding them relate all these things to the Church—that is, the disciples at Jerusalem—he went away to another place, that he might be out of the reach of Herod.

At daybreak, there was no small stir among the soldiers when they found their prisoner missing; and Herod was so enraged with them for letting Peter go, as he supposed they had done, that he ordered the guards to be put to death.

Elymas Struck Blind

THE Jews who lived in Damascus were so angry with Saul for proving that Jesus was the Messiah, that the next time he came to the city they plotted together to kill him. And they kept watch night and day at the gates of the city, that they might be sure to catch him.

But Saul knew of their wicked design; and his friends got him safely out, by letting him down in a basket through the window of a house that was built upon the wall.

Then he went up to Jerusalem, where the disciples, knowing how he had formerly persecuted them, were at first afraid of having any thing to do with him. But Barnabas, one of the disciples who had been at Damascus, took him to Peter and James, and told them how the Lord Jesus Himself had appeared to Saul, and chosen him to be one of His apostles. Then they received him, and he staid with them, till he was obliged, in order to save his life, to go away to his own city, Tarsus, where he lived for some years.

Afterward he and Barnabas traveled through various countries, teaching the people about Jesus Christ. One of the places to which they went was Cyprus, a large island in the Mediterranean Sea, and the birthplace of Barnabas. Here the Roman governor, Sergius Paulus, sent for the apostles, that they might tell him about God and Jesus Christ. And when he heard them, he thought that what they said must be true. But there was a man with him named Elymas, who was what in those days was called a sorcerer—that is, one who pretended to be a prophet, and to be able to do wonderful things, almost like the miracles that God enabled His prophets and disciples to do. And this man did all that he could to prevent the Roman governor's becoming a Christian.

But Paul (for so Saul was then called) was bidden by God Himself to put an end to the wicked doings of Elymas. So, looking steadily at him, he spoke to him sternly of his misdeeds, telling him that God was about to punish them by causing him to be quite blind for a time. As he spoke, a mist came over the eyes of Elymas; and then it was all dark, so that he was obliged to seek some one to lead him.

Then, when the Roman governor saw that Elymas was struck blind by God, as Paul had said he should be, he was filled with astonishment, and believed all that the apostles had taught him about the true God, and Jesus Christ His Son.

Paul at Jerusalem

PAUL often got very ill-treated as he went about teaching. He was beaten, he was put in prison, he was stoned, till the people thought he was dead; indeed, over and over again the Jews would have murdered him if they could.

Once when he and Silas were in prison, praying and singing hymns to God, and while the other prisoners were listening to them, there was suddenly such a great earthquake that the very foundations of the prison were shaken. Immediately all the doors were opened and the chains that bound all the prisoners were loosened.

When the jailer suddenly awoke and saw the prison doors wide open, he drew his sword and was about to kill himself, thinking that the prisoners had escaped.

But Paul shouted to him that they were still there, and the jailer rushed in and threw himself on his knees before Paul, begging him to tell how he might be saved.

They answered, "Believe in the Lord Jesus Christ and you and all your household will be saved."

So Paul and Silas preached the word of the Lord to him and all his family, and the jailer took them at that very hour of the night and washed and bathed their wounds. Then the jailer and his family were baptized, and took Paul and Silas into their home and gave them food to eat.

In the morning there was an order from the city officials which said, "Release these men."

The last time that Paul was in Jerusalem, finding him in the Temple, some of the Jews who hated Paul laid hold of him, dragged him out to kill him, and raised such a riot in the city that the captain of the guard was obliged to bring out a company of soldiers to put an end to it.

When the people saw the soldiers, they were frightened, and left off beating Paul. But when the captain asked what their prisoner had done wrong, they clamored, and became so riotous again that he was obliged to order the guard to take Paul into the castle, close to the Temple, for safety.

When Paul was on the staircase leading from the Temple into the castle, he begged the captain to let him speak to the people. And then he told them how Jesus Christ had appeared to him as he went to Damascus, and that He had commanded him to tell the Gentiles that He was their Savior, and not the Savior of the Jews only. When Paul said this, the multitude broke out in fresh rage against him; for the Jews thought that God did not care for any people but themselves. And they clamored so for his being put to death, that the captain (who, being a Roman, did not understand what Paul had been saying to the Jews in their own language) ordered him to be brought into the castle and beaten, to make him confess what he had done wrong.

But when the soldiers were going to beat him, Paul told them that, though he was a Jew, he was a Roman citizen. They were afraid when they heard this, for it was against the law either to beat or put fetters upon a Roman citizen; so they brought him to the chief priests, that he might defend himself against what the Jews had to say of him. But the chief priests, and those with them, quarreled so violently among themselves after they had heard Paul, that the chief captain was again obliged to send soldiers to take him into the castle, lest he should be torn to pieces.

Paul was safe in the castle; but the Jews laid a plan to kill him the next time he was brought out before the chief priests. Paul's nephew heard of this, and told it to the chief captain, who then sent Paul away, with a guard of near five hundred soldiers, horse and foot, to Caesarea, where Felix, the governor, was.

Paul at Melita

PAUL at length found that there was little chance of his being justly treated if he were tried in his own country; so, as he was a Roman citizen, he required that he should be sent to Rome, that the emperor himself might judge him.

It was a long and dangerous voyage from Judea to Italy. The vessel in which Paul and a number of other prisoners were sailing thither crept slowly along in the Mediterranean Sea, going this way and that, according as the wind blew; for sailors in those days could not manage vessels as they do now, neither had they any compass to direct them. Suddenly a violent storm arose, which almost wrecked the ship at once. But, by throwing overboard the tackling of the ship, and its lading, they managed to struggle on for a time. But presently, trying to steer the vessel into what seemed a safe opening in the shore, they ran it aground; and the forepart sticking fast, the stern was soon broken to pieces by the waves dashing against it.

Then the soldiers proposed to kill all the prisoners, lest, in the confusion, they should make their escape. But the

Paul in prison.

Roman officer, who had charge of Paul and the others, would not allow this. He ordered all who could swim to throw themselves into the sea, and get to land as well as they could. Those who could not swim he told to cling to planks and broken pieces of the ship, which would float them ashore. And so they all got safe to land.

The island on which they were shipwrecked was named Melita, but is now called Malta. And though the people who lived in it were rude and uncivilized, they treated the poor, wet, cold, weary crew very kindly, lighting a fire to warm them, and doing what they could to comfort them. They all had to set to work, and Paul collected a heap of wood for the fire. But when he threw it upon the fire, the heat caused a viper, which had been hidden among the wood, to come out, and it fastened upon his hand. When the poor, ignorant people saw this, they thought Paul must be some very wicked man, who was to be stung to death for his ill deeds. But when, instead of falling down dead, as they expected, they saw him shake the viper off into the fire, and remain unhurt, they changed their minds, and thought him a god!

Paul did many miracles at Melita. And when at length he sailed away to Italy, he taught the people of Rome, both Jews and Gentiles, that Jesus Christ was the Savior of the world.

Philip and the Ethiopian

WHEN Stephen was stoned to death, a great persecution broke out against the church in Jerusalem, and many of the disciples scattered in different directions and went about spreading the good news about Jesus.

Philip went to the city of Samaria, where he told about Christ and performed many miracles. Many who were sick and lame were healed, and they in turn went about telling their belief in great joy.

Then an angel came to Philip and said, "Rise, and go south along the desert road from Jerusalem to Gaza."

On his way he met an Ethiopian who had charge of the treasures of the queen. He was sitting in his chariot by the roadside reading from the prophet Isaiah, and the angel said to Philip, "Go up and speak to the man in the chariot."

So Philip went and heard him reading from the prophet, and he asked the man whether he understood that which he was reading.

The Ethiopian said, "How can I understand when there is no one to tell me what it means?"

Then Philip got up and sat beside him in the chariot, explaining to him and telling him about Jesus.

After a while the chariot stopped by a stream of water, and the Ethiopian said, "Here is water now. What is there to prevent my being baptized?"

So he was baptized at once, and Philip went on his way rejoicing.